TAV SCHOOL

of

HEALING MANUAL

〜⁕〜

GLORIA JOHNSON

authorHOUSE°

AuthorHouse™
1663 Liberty Drive
Bloomington, IN 47403
www.authorhouse.com
Phone: 1 (800) 839-8640

Published by AuthorHouse 11/28/2016

ISBN: 978-1-5246-4473-4 (sc)
ISBN: 978-1-5246-4472-7 (e)

Print information available on the last page.

Any people depicted in stock imagery provided by Thinkstock are models, and such images are being used for illustrative purposes only. Certain stock imagery © Thinkstock.

This book is printed on acid-free paper.

Because of the dynamic nature of the Internet, any web addresses or links contained in this book may have changed since publication and may no longer be valid. The views expressed in this work are solely those of the author and do not necessarily reflect the views of the publisher, and the publisher hereby disclaims any responsibility for them.

KJV
Scripture quotations marked KJV are from the Holy Bible, King James Version (Authorized Version). First published in 1611. Quoted from the KJV Classic Reference Bible, Copyright © 1983 by The Zondervan Corporation.

CONTENTS

Contents

ACKNOWLEDGMENT

This healing manual is dedicated to my Mother, Pastor Obelia Manson. Mom I am so blessed to have had the opportunity to witness the healing anointing flowing through you as a child. Because of this anointing, as a child I never experience doctors visit accept for checkups. God was faithful to heal through your hands. I remember as a child wanting to experience being hospitalized. Now this was a foolish wish, nevertheless I desired very much to visit the hospital. Well, I made up this story that help my wish come true. I had a popped out belly button that was harmless and never had caused me any pain. I complained that I was in extreme pain. Well, my story worked and off to the hospital I went. Of course the doctors found nothing, so I was taken back home. I was now satisfied to have had my wish granted. Later after I was grown, I admitted the truth to my parents. I didn't realize then the blessing of enjoying good health. I now greatly value the healing anointing that still flows through my Mother at 83 years of age. I am also honored that God has chosen me as a vessel that his healing anointing flows through today! Mom I praise God for the example you have set as a woman of God. It has greatly influence my life!

INTRODUCTION

This healing manual is written for those who desire healing in any area of their lives. It is God's will that we are whole in every area of our lives. 1 Thessalonians 5:23 states, And the very God of peace sanctify you wholly, (complete, perfect) and I pray God your whole spirit and soul and body be preserved blameless unto the coming of our Lord Jesus Christ. Jesus has already paid the price for our healing. Now we must receive it, begin to walk in the healing he has provided. This manual will help build your faith. Romans 10:17 states, so then faith cometh by hearing and hearing by the word of God. Many times God's people are receiving healing, but are failing to maintain their healing. Hosea 4:6 states, My people are destroyed for a lack of knowledge. In lesson's 1,2 and 3 we will examine how to obtain your healing and in lesson 4 we will examine the power of the word and healing promises. We will also examine in lesson 5 how to maintain healings you have obtained; we will talk about wholeness for the total you. Each story in lesson's 1,2 and 3 will be narrated.

The importance of faith

Faith is a very important ingredient that will help one to become whole. Mark 9:23 says; If thou canst believe all things are possible to him that believe. So let's begin by looking at 6 scriptures that speaks of faith. The first scripture defines what faith is.

(1)   Romans 4: 13,20,21

> 13 For the promise, that he should be the heir of the world, was not to Abraham, or to his seed, through the law, but through the righteousness of faith.

20 He (Abraham) staggered not at the promise of God through unbelief, but was strong in faith, giving glory to God;

21 And being fully persuaded that, what he had promised, he was able to perform.

One can understand from this scripture that Abraham was a man who had strong faith. He believed the promise God made regarding him regarding becoming a heir of the world. He was able to have a celebration before ever seeing any manifestation. So how was Abraham able to keep his faith strong? Verse 21 tells us the answer. Abraham became fully persuaded that everything God had promise him, God would perform. So we can define faith this way. Faith is becoming fully persuaded whatever God has promise you, God will perform!

(2) Hebrew 11:6 Without faith it is impossible to please him (God) for he that cometh to God must believe that he is, and that he is a rewarder of them that diligently seek him.

One can understand from this scripture, first of all, that God is a God that honors faith. In fact, he requires it. The scripture says without faith it is impossible to please God. Secondly the scripture goes on to say, for he that cometh to God must believe that God is. So when one comes to God, they must believe that God exist, and the scripture goes on to say; and that he is a rewarder of them that diligently seek him. The word diligently means to search, seek out. So we can also understand that God will reward those who will seek him out.

(3) Romans 12:3 For I say through the grace given unto me, to every man that is among you not to think of himself more highly than he ought to think, but to think soberly according as God hath dealth (given) to every man the measure of faith. Our meditation will be on the later part of this scripture, but to think soberly according as God hath dealth to every man the measure of faith.

One can understand from this scripture that God has given every believer the measure of faith. Now the faith God has given every believer is capable of meeting every need if one exercises their faith properly. In order for one to exercise their faith properly, one faith must be kept strong.

(4)   Romans 10:17 Faith cometh by hearing and hearing by the word of God.

We can better understand this scripture by saying our faith comes, or is set in motion upon hearing a word from God, if you believe it!

But now once again that faith must be kept strong, one must take that word, believe it and begin to meditate upon that word.

Meditate-mutter, mumble, ponder, think deeply, reflect upon.

Meditation is very necessary because you have an enemy who wants to steal the word. John 10:10 The thief (devil) cometh not, but to steal, kill and destroy. Mark 4:15 Speaks of the parable of the sower. Jesus says when the word is sown immediately the enemy comes after the word. So one should meditate the word of God until it is rooted (seeded) in the heart, if the word is properly meditated upon, it will come out of the mouth in your hour of temptation when the enemy shows up. Jesus spoke the word during his hour of temptation and the devil left. (Matt.4:1-11) Matthew 12:34 says; Out of the abundance (over flow) of the heart the mouth speaketh.

Now powerful results happen when the word is meditated. Joshua 1:8 helps us to understand the power of meditation. It states;

This book of the law (word of God) shall not depart out of thy mouth, but thou shalt meditate there-in day and night, that thou mayest observe to do according to all that is written there-in. For then thou shalt make thou way prosperous and then thou shalt have good success.

(5)   2 Corinthians 5:7 For we walk by faith, not by sight.

We can understand from this scripture, that we, God's children are to live by faith (make it a life-style) and not be moved by sight, our senses what we see, hear or feel.

(6)   Galatians 5:6 For in Jesus Christ neither circumcision availeth anything nor uncircumcision, but faith which worketh by love.

Our meditation will be on the later part of this scripture, Faith which worketh by love.

One should understand from this scripture that when one has a healthy perspective of God's love, it will help one faith to operate effectively. What is a healthy perspective of the love of God? One should understand two things about God's love. (1) One should first understand they are loved by God with an everlasting love. (Jeremiah 31:3) A unconditional love, God loves us in spite of our short comings and failures. If one doesn't understand the love that God has for them, it will effect one ability to extend God's love toward their fellow man. One must know God is not holding on to your past failures, if we confess our sins to God, he is faithful and just to forgive us of our sins and to cleanse us from all unrighteousness. (1John 1:9)

(2) One should also understand, you and I have been given a charge to walk in God's love toward our fellow man.

John 13:34 Jesus said; A new commandment I give unto you, that ye love one-another as I have loved you, that ye also love one-another.

So the disciples had a healthy perspective of the love of God. They understood they were loved by God despite their short comings. Jesus demonstrated this unto them. They also understood they had been given a charge to walk in the love of God toward their fellow man.

Understand the love of God has been shed abroad in your hearts by the holy ghost according to Romans 5:5b We who have had our spirits reborn have the ability to love like God. Jude 1:21 Tells us to keep ourselves in the love of God.

So since love helps one faith to operate more effectively, it is important to understand what love really is. 1Corinthians 13:4-8 defines what love really is. There are 15 characteristics traits of love and I really want to help you understand what kind of love God loves you and me with and the kind of love that has been shed abroad in our hearts by the holy ghost. I have written the definition of love coming from both the King James version and the Amplified version. Now the amplified version does just that, it amplifies, brings greater clarity to the meaning.

The word charity is used in the KJV but the Greek word for charity is agape, which means love.

15 Characteristics Traits of Love

(1) Love suffereth long and is kind.
     AMP. Love endures long and is patient and kind.

(2) Love envieth not.
     AMP. Love never is envious, nor boils over with jealousy.

(3) Love vaunteth not itself.
     Amp Love is not boastful or vain-glorious.

(4) Love is not puffed up.
     Amp Love does not display itself haughtily, it is not conceited (arrogant and inflated with pride).

(5) Love doeth not behave itself unseemly.
     AMP. Love is not rude (unmannerly and does not act unbecoming).

(6) Love seeketh not her own.
     Amp. Love does not insist on its own rights or its own way, for it is not self-seeking.

(7) Love is not easily provoked.
     Amp Love is not touchy or fretful or resentful.

(8) Love thinketh no evil.
     AMP Love takes no account of the evil done to it.
     (it pays no attention to a suffered wrong)

(9)   Love rejoiceth not in iniquity.
      AMP Love does not rejoice at injustice and unrighteousness.

(10) Love rejoices in truth.
      AMP. Love rejoices when right and truth prevails.

(11) Love beareth all things.
      Amp. Love bears up under anything and everything that comes.

(12) Love believeth all things.
      Amp. Love is ever ready to believe the best of every person.

(13) Love hopeth all things.
      Amp. Love hopes are fadeless under all circumstances.

(14) Love endureth all things.
      Amp. Love endureth everything without weakening.

(15) Love never fails.
      AMP. Love never fades out or becomes obsolete or comes to an end.

This type of love (Agape) if one has a healthy perspective of God's love, will help one faith to work more effectively. It will help to protect one faith.

Now let's review our 6 scriptures that speaks of faith.

1.   Romans 4: 13,20,21

     13 For the promise, that he should be the heir of the world, was not to Abraham, or to his seed, through the law, but through the righteousness of faith.

     20 He (Abraham) staggered not at the promises of God through unbelief; but was strong in faith, giving glory to God;

     21 And being fully persuaded that, what he had promised, he was able also to perform.

We define faith this way; one becoming fully persuaded that what God has promised, he is able also to perform.

2. Hebrews 11:6 Without faith it is impossible to please him. For he that cometh to God must believe that he is, and that he is a rewarder of them that diligently seek him.

3. Romans 12:3b God has dealt to every man the measure of faith.

4. Romans 10:17 Faith cometh by hearing and hearing by the word of God.

5. 2 Corinthians 5:7 For we walk by faith not by sight.

6. Galatians 5:6b Faith which worketh by love.

Now let's continue our lesson on faith.

Now faith begins where the will of God is known. The will of God is the word of God. So faith begins where the word of God is known or revealed. Let's look at an example that will help you better understand God's word is his will.

Let's say someone is in need of healing and they are wondering, is God a healer? and if so, does he want me healed? Well the word of God says this…

Isaiah 53:5 But he (Jesus) was wounded for our transgressions he was bruised for our iniquities, the chastisement of our peace was upon him, and with his stripes we are healed.

1Peter 2:24 Who his own self bare our sins in his own body on the tree, that we being dead to sin should live unto righteousness, by whose stripes ye were healed.

Exodus 15:26b For I am the Lord that healeth thee.

So we see God is a healer, he believed in healing so much that he gave the life of his only son. We also understand that God wants to heal you, according to Exodus 15:26b

Now we will examine individuals who operated their faith properly and those who did not. We will also examine some other hindrance that can prevent one faith from operating properly or remaining strong. Lastly will look at individuals who exercised great faith. We will look to see the characteristic traits of love that helped their faith to operate more effectively, because we understand according to Galatians 5:6b Faith worketh by love.

Now understand the individuals we will examine are all under the old covenant. We now have a better covenant with better promises. (Hebrews 8:6) So we have an advantage the old testament believers didn't partake of. Understand under the old covenant, the love of God was not yet shed abroad in the hearts of these believers. Only after Jesus ascended into heaven did the holy spirit indwell the hearts of believers during the day of Pentecost. But, these old covenant believers did understand they were loved by God with an everlasting love. (Jeremiah 31:3) And they understood they were to love their neighbors as themselves. (Leviticus 19:18)

Lesson 1

ILLUSTRATIONS OF UNBELIF

Now just as faith can accelerate a move of God, unbelief can stop or shut down a move of God. Let's define the word unbelief.

Unbelief- A lack of belief because of insufficient evidence.

Remember faith needs no evidence, faith believes in spite of evidence, according to Hebrews 11:1 Now faith is the substance of things hope for, the evidence of things not seen.

Hebrews 3:19 says; So we see they could not enter in, because of unbelief.

Amp. Ver. So we see they were not able to enter in because unbelief had shut them out.

There is a difference between doubt and unbelief.

Doubt- one is of 2 different opinions, they believe one minute and the next minute they are doubting.

Unbelief- one remains of the same opinion consistently, they just don't believe.

Our first story comes from Numbers 13:1-3 and verses17-33 I have entitled this story "Unbelief stop the children of Israel from entering their promise land" I will narrate each story.

1 God gives Moses some instructions.

2 Here are the instructions, he tells Moses to send 12 men, leaders of their tribes, to search the land of Canaan he says, the land which I given unto the children of Israel.

Now here is the word of the Lord. According to Rom. 10:17 Faith comes (set in motion) by hearing God's word. One must now take that word believe it and then begin to meditate on that word begin to speak it. This should have been the twelve men meditations, but let's continue our story.

3 Moses obey, he sends out the twelve men from the wilderness of Paran, who were each heads of their tribes.

4-16 Tells the name of the men and the names of the tribes they are from.

17 Moses gives directions how to enter the land of Canaan, he says go southward into the mountains.

18 Moses then tells them a couple of things to check on in the land, he says, see what the land is. Check out the people, see if they are weak or strong, few or many;

19 Check out the condition of the land, see if it is good or bad, check out the cities, see if the people live in tents or strong-holds.

20 He says, check the land, see if it is fat or lean and if there is wood. He then instructs them to be of good courage (brave, fearless) and bring back some fruit from the land. Now the time was the time of the first ripe grapes.

The men now have 2 words that should have been meditated upon,

(1) God has given you the land (2) Be of good courage, (don't fear) bring back fruit.

21-24 The men leave; they search the land from the wilderness of Zin to Rehob. They then come up by the south and came to Hebron where the children of Anak lived. They continue their journey until they come unto the brook of Eshcol, they now cut down a branch with one cluster of grapes, carrying it on a pole between two of them, also bringing back some pomegranates and figs. Now the place was called the brook of Eschcol because of the cluster of grapes the children of Israel cut down.

25 The men now return home after searching the land for 40 days.

26 The men report back to Moses and Aaron and all the congregation of the children of Israel, they show them the fruit from the land.

27 Here is their report, they said the land you sent us to, floweth with milk and honey and this is the fruit. (so it is a good land, their report is good so far).

28 They state, nevertheless (however or but) the people are strong that dwell in the land and the cities are walled (fortified) strong walls of protection, and a very large land, they continue to say; and there we saw the children of Anak who were giants.

So here is unbelief, their faith is now challenged by what they saw. We understand, we are to walk by faith not by sight. (2 Corinthians 5:7) God was very much aware of the people that were in the land. He knew there were strong walls that surrounded the people. The men should have meditated the word given by God, that God had has given you the land and be of good courage, (don't fear) and bring back fruit. Had this word been meditated properly, it would have been in their hearts and now coming out of their mouths despite the present circumstances.

29 The men go on to tell of other nations that dwell there, they state; The Amalekites dwell in the land of the south. The Hittites, Jebusites

and the Amorites dwell in the mountains and the Canaanites dwell by the sea, by the coast of Jordan.

30 Caleb also one of the twelve men, calms down the people before Moses, he says; let us go up at once and possess the land, for we are well able to overcome the land.

God has given every man the measure of faith (Romans12:3) Caleb is exercising his, the other men allow unbelief to cause them not to believe God's word, in their eyes there is insufficient evidence to take the land, that's unbelief. Understand all these men saw the very same thing, but what cause Caleb to have a different spirit? Caleb meditated upon the word of God spoken to them, it was now safely in his heart, so out of the abundance of his heart his mouth now speaks. (Matthew 12:34)

31 The other men still insisted, we are not able to go up against the people for they are strong.

32 The men chose to ignore Caleb's report and deliver an evil report, persuading the children of Israel to doubt the word of the Lord. They state, the land devours its' inhabitants, and the men are men of great stature.

33 They continues to say, there we saw the giants, the sons of Anak, and we were in our own sight as grasshoppers, and so we were in their sight.

In other words, not only did these men feel inadequate, they saw themselves as grasshoppers, they also felt the Canaanites viewed them in this manner as well. Proverbs 23:7 says; As he (man) thinketh in heart, so is he. The children of Israel forgot what God had spoken, they should have meditated upon the word of God. So we see they did not enter into the land God had promised, because unbelief shut down the move of God! (Numbers 14:23)

Now let's look at more hindrances to one faith.

Let's talk about forgivingness (Mark 11:20-26)

Sometimes holding on to offences can hinder your faith from operating properly. Gal.5:6b says, Faith worketh by love.

20 And in the morning, as they passed by, they saw the fig tree dried up from the roots.

21 And Peter calling to remembrance saith unto him (Jesus) master, behold, the fig tree which thou cursedst is withered away.

22 And Jesus answering saith unto them, have faith in God.

23 For verily I say unto you, that whosoever shall say unto this mountain, be thou removed, and be thou cast into the sea; and shall not doubt in his heart, but shall believe that those things which he saith shall come to pass, he shall have whatsoever he saith.

24 Therefore I say unto you, what things so ever ye desire, when you pray, believe that ye receive them, and ye shall have them.

25 And when ye stand praying, forgive, if ye have aught against any; that your Father also which is in heaven may forgive you your trespasses.

26 But if ye do not forgive, neither will your Father which is in heaven forgive your trespasses.

Notice verse 25 begins with the conjunction and. A conjunction connects a sentence; it is a thought being continued. Jesus gave them the understanding that holding on to offences can hinder one faith as well as prayers and here is why; when one is praying and not seeing results, one may tend to think God is not hearing their prayers which could affect their faith. We must learn to forgive ourselves as well as others. Understand holding on to offences can cause all kind of sickness in the body. God made the body and he didn't create no place to store offenses.

Ephesians 4:26 Be ye angry and sin not, let not the sun go down on your wrath.

Don't store negative emotions. Now let's look at the story of Joseph. I will give you a brief summary of the story of Joseph. This story demonstrates the power of forgiveness. You can read the story and its' entirety found in Genesis chapters' 37-50.

Joseph was badly mistreated by his brothers. His brothers were envious of him, because his Father favored him. He was the son of his father's old age. God gave Joseph 2 dreams. He shared the dreams with his brothers' and father. The dreams were both prophetic words regarding Joseph's destiny. His brothers became envious of him. The word says they hated him more because of the dreams. Both dreams showed Joseph in a place of authority over his brethren. One day his brothers decided to get rid of Joseph. They sold him to some Ishmeelites. Joseph became a slave and suffered much hardship; finally, the season came where God exalted Joseph. He became a ruler over all Egypt. He was second in command next to the Pharaoh. Meanwhile there was a famine all over the land. It even hit the land of Canaan where Joseph brothers were. No one had food but Egypt. Joseph brothers had to come to Joseph to receive food. They became afraid when they knew Joseph was the head guy in charge of the land. Joseph could have harbor (stored) bitterness, held on to the offences done by his brethren. He could have chosen not to forgive them, but this is what the word of God says Joseph told his brothers. He said don't be grieved or angry with yourselves, that it was God who sent him to Egypt to preserve their lives. This very statement tells us Joseph had forgiven his brothers. God gave Joseph 2 sons in the land of Egypt. He named his first born, Mannaseh; which means one who causes to forget, for Joseph said God has made (help me) forget all my toils and all my father house; referring to the wrong he had suffered in his fathers' house.

God will help you forget (release) your past hurts and failures but we must hear and obey what he has instructed us to do. Joseph named the other son Ephramin; which means fruitful for Joseph said God has caused me to be fruitful in the land of my afflictions. Joseph became fruitful (prosperous) because he didn't get stuck in his past.

God wants all his children to be fruitful (prosperous) but we must forgive, don't get stuck in your past, allow God to turn the evil done unto you into a blessing. If we would forgive (forget the past) refuse to continue to rehearse the former things, God is able to do a new thing in your life.

Isaiah 43:18, 19

> 18 Remember you not the former things (don't rehearse them or keep recalling them) neither consider the things of old.

> 19 Behold I will do a new thing. Now it shall spring forth. Shall ye not know it. I will even make a way in the wilderness and rivers in the desert.

Some people can't embrace the new things because they won't release the former things.

If we would be willing to forgive (release the past) God will cause us to be fruitful, to move forward into all the blessings he has for us.

Matthew 5:44 Tells us 4 things to do unto our enemies. They are;

> (1) Love them (2) Bless them (3) Do good unto them (4) Pray for them

Jesus tells us in Luke 17:1,2

> 1 It is impossible but that offences will come: but woe unto him, through whom they come.

> 2 It were better for him that a millstone were hanged about his neck, and he cast into the sea, that that he should offend one of these little ones.

Offences will come, but woe to that man who offends.

God doesn't take offences lightly, allow God to judge your offenders.

Illustrations of faith

Mark 5:21-43 Now here are two stories where both individuals exercised their faith properly.

"The daughter of Jarius at the point of death and The woman with an issue of blood"

21 Jesus enters into a ship and passes over to the other side, many people are gathering around him.

22 A man by the name of Jarius who is a ruler of the synagogue, meets Jesus and falls at his feet.

Understand his faith probably could have come by hearing testimonies about Jesus. No doubt he believed and meditated on the words he had heard.

23 Jarius now tells Jesus his problem, he says his daughter is at the point of death, but more importantly here is his faith, He says come lay hands on her and she will be healed and live.

Jarius is exercising his faith, God's given man the measure of faith. (Romans 12:3)

24 Jesus is in agreement, no problem Jarius is using his faith, Jesus goes with him and many people crowded him, following along.

25 Jesus begins his journey, he runs into another problem, a woman who has an issue of blood for twelve years.

26 This woman has been to many doctors and spent all her money, but the word says, she hadn't gotten better, but rather had grown worse.

27 The woman had heard about Jesus, she now presses her way through the crowd of people and touches the hem of Jesus' garment.

Understand this woman faith had probably come from hearing testimonies about Jesus, she had taken those words, believe them and begin to meditate upon those words.

28 Now here is her faith she is exercising, she says, If I may but touch his clothes, I will be whole.

Now there was a reason this woman didn't want attention drawn to her. She had an issue, a flow of blood, and according to the levitical law (Leviticus 15:25) she wasn't supposed to be in the public eye.

29 The word says immediately the blood dries up and she feels in her body she has been healed.

Understand her faith carried her unto her manifestation, your faith can carry you to your manifestation but it must be guarded from doubt and fear. This woman probably didn't discuss what she was intending to do with no-one because they probably would have discouraged her, because according to the levitical law she was not supposed to be in the public eye.

30 The woman probably was ready to turn and leave the scene, but the word says Jesus felt virtue (power) going out of him, he turns around and ask the question, who touched my clothes?

Understand our faith can release power from God!

31 The disciples don't quite understand Jesus' question, they reply, there are multitudes of people around you, and how will you ask, who touch me?

32 Jesus looks around and sees the woman.

33 The woman then comes fearing and trembling, knowing what had happened in her, falls down before Jesus and confesses everything that had happen.

34 Jesus then tells the woman, daughter, your faith has made you whole, go in peace, and be whole of your plague.

35 Mean while there came from the ruler of the synagogue's house a message; which said, your daughter is dead, why trouble the master any further?

36 As soon as Jesus heard the words that was spoken, he quickly intervenes, he then speaks five faith filled words to the ruler of the synagogue, he says, be not afraid, only believe.

Jesus understood just as faith comes by hearing God's word; fear, doubt, and unbelief can come by words as well, and God honors' faith. Jesus wanted Jarius faith to stay strong.

Understand fear hinders' faith, Jarius now have the word of the Lord to meditate upon, he is now strengthen; he takes courage, pondering, meditating upon these words, Be not afraid, only believe, he then continues his journey.

37 Jesus knows at this point all doubt, fear and unbelief must go. He doesn't allow the crowd to continue with him. The word says he allows only Peter, James and John.

Understand, God honors' faith and without faith it is impossible to please God. Hebrews 11:6

38 Jesus makes his arrival to the house of the ruler. He views the situation, here is what he finds. There is crying, wailing and a lot of confusion.

39 Jesus enters the room, he now asks' a question; and then makes a profound statement, he ask, why are you weeping and carrying on this way? He then makes the ever profound statement, he says the girl is not dead, but sleepeth.

Understand Jesus sees this girl through the eyes of faith. Unbelief is no-where in the picture.

40 The people begin to mock him, they laughed him to scorn, that located their faith, they are exercising none. They don't believe. Jesus

puts them out and takes with him the father and mother, along with his disciples and enters the room where the girl is lying, he gets rid of all doubt and unbelief.

Understand you too must take necessary precautions to guard your faith as well, everybody may not agree with your faith.

41 Jesus then takes the girl by the hand, and says, damsel, I say unto you arise.

Jesus treats the girl as if she were asleep. He takes her by the hand and says arise.

42 The word says immediately the girl arises and walk, she is twelve years of age. The people are astonished. (they are amazed)

43 Jesus then instructs them not to share this with any one, but to give the girl something to eat.

One should understand in both cases, the woman with the issue of blood and Jarius daughter being raised up from her death bed, that faith was responsible for the manifestation (evidence) we now read about.

One must carefully guard their faith; it must be kept strong.

Illustrations of those who exercised great faith

"The woman of Canaan" Matthew 15:21-28

Jesus stated in this story that this woman exercised great faith, so we will examine to see if we can find any characteristics traits of love demonstrated by this Canaanite woman, because we understand according to Galatians 5:6b, Faith worketh by love. When one has a healthy perspective of God's love, they understand they are loved by God and they have the responsibility to extend God's love toward their fellow man.

21 Jesus now departs from the coasts of Tyre and Sidon.

22 A woman of Canaan approaches him, here is her desperate cry, she says have mercy on me, O Lord thou son of David, my daughter is grievously vexed (troubled) with a devil.

This woman's' faith probably came by hearing testimonies about Jesus. Remember faith can come (able to be set in motion) by hearing a word from God. (Romans 10:17)

23 After the woman makes this desperate plead, Jesus seemly ignores her, so much to the point the disciples saw her as annoying, and they encourage Jesus, just send her away.

24 Jesus finally responds' he says; I am sent to the lost sheep of Israel (referring to the children of Israel).

25 The woman's faith is not moved, she's not discouraged, she instead worship Jesus and pleads for his help.

26 Jesus responds again, he says; It is not meet (right or fair) to take the children bread (referring to the children of Israel) and cast it to the dogs. (referring to the Canaanite woman)

27 This woman still isn't moved, she's not offended, but agrees with Jesus, she says truth Lord, but the dogs (referring to her-self) eat the crumbs which falls from their master's table. (referring to the Israelites)

28 Jesus now responds to the woman he says; O woman great is your faith. He then tells her, be it unto thee even as thou wilt. (wish) And the word says; her daughter was made whole from that very hour.

Now let's examine this woman's faith, let's see if we can find any characteristics traits of love demonstrated by this woman, because remember Galatians 5:6b says, Faith works by love. Understand, when one understands they are loved by God, they can then extend God's love toward their fellow man.

Now one may say this woman was desperate, so she was willing to do anything, there may be some truth to that, but this woman still exhibited God's love.

I've chosen 3 characteristics traits of love demonstrated by this Canaanite woman. Understand if this woman didn't understand she was loved by God, her faith could have possibly been hindered to trust God.

Remember these believers we are examining are all under the old covenant, although it is in the new testament. Jesus had not yet died, so the love of God was not shed abroad in their hearts by the holy spirit, but they understood they were loved by God with a everlasting love, according to Jeremiah 31:3 and they understood they were to love their neighbors as themselves according to Leviticus 19:18.

Let's now review the 3 characteristics traits of love that can be seen demonstrated by this Canaanite woman.

1. Love doeth not behave itself unseemly.

    Amp Ver. Love is not rude (unmannerly and does not act unbecomingly.

    Can we find this trait of love demonstrated by the Canaanite woman? Yes, many opportunities were presented unto this woman to behave in an unseemly (rude way) but she made the choice to demonstrate God's love. She understood she was loved by God and she trusted him, and she also extended the love of God toward her fellowman. Let's examine 3 opportunities that were presented to her, where she could have behaved in an unseemly way (rude way).

    (1) verse 23, when this woman makes her desperate plead to Jesus, he seemly ignores her, so much to the point the disciples sees her as annoying, they suggest to Jesus just send her away!

    So here was an opportunity she could have responded in a rude way toward the disciples and Jesus, but she didn't.

    (2) In verse 24, When Jesus finally did answer, he responded by saying he was called to the lost sheep of Israel, she was a Canaanite. So here was another opportunity she could have become rude, but she didn't.

(3) In verse 26, When Jesus referred to her as a dog, he said it wasn't fair to take the children bread and cast it to the dogs. She most definitely could have become rude, but she didn't. This woman must have understood she was loved by God and she continues to extend God's love toward her fellowman. Her faith was protected by the love she understood.

2. Love is not easily provoked.

Amp. Ver. Love is not touchy or fretful or resentful.

Can this trait of love be seen demonstrated by the Canaanite woman?

Yes, once again in verse 23, when Jesus seemly ignores this woman after she makes her plead, he then acknowledges her presence, he says in verse 24, I am sent to the lost sheep of Israel, in other words you are a Canaanite and I am sent to the Israelites, had this woman been easily provoked touchy or fretful, she could have easily come to the conclusion that Jesus was prejudice and left the scene. But she must have understood she was loved by God and she continues to trust God, therefore her faith was protected by the love she understood.

3. Love thinketh no evil.

Amp. Ver. Love takes no account of the evil done to it. It pays no attention to a suffered wrong.

Can we find this trait of love demonstrated by this Canaanite woman? Absolutely, we can truly acknowledge this characteristics trait being demonstrated by this Canaanite woman. Let's examine our story once again. In verse 26 when Jesus referred to this woman as a dog, she could have at this point kept account of everything Jesus had spoken to her. She could have chosen to think evil of him but she didn't. Let's review her many opportunities.

(1) In verse 23, when Jesus seemly ignores this woman, she could have begun to keep an account or record of what she seen as evil. She could have said ok, strike 1, Jesus has ignored me, he really must don't care.

(2) In verse 24, when Jesus finally respond to this woman, he informs her he was called to the Israelites, she was a Canaanite. She could have been still keeping an account of what she perceived as evil, and thought ok, strike 2, Jesus appears to be prejudice.

(3) In verse 26, Now Jesus refers to her as a dog, she could have kept account and said strike 3, now Jesus this is it, I am done with you, and left the scene.

But this woman response to Jesus when he referred to her as dog, she says, truth Lord, but the dogs eat the crumbs that falls from their masters' table.

In other- words she confident she was loved by God, and her attitude was, if I am a dog, dogs are entitled to something, they don't leave empty. They eat the crumbs that fall from their masters' table.

Jesus then responds; O woman, great is your faith. This woman knew she was loved by God and she trusted him. She also extended the love of God toward her fellowman. Her faith was protected by the love she understood.

Understand, we too must remember, whatever we need from God, God wants us to use our faith and our faith works by love.

Lesson 2

Now let's review our 6 scriptures that speaks of faith

1. Romans 4: 13,20,21

    13 For the promise, that he should be the heir of the world, was not to Abraham, or to his seed, through the law, but through the righteousness of faith.

    20 He (Abraham) staggered not at the promises of God through unbelief; but was strong in faith, giving glory to God;

    21 And being fully persuaded that, what he had promised, he was able also to perform.

    We define faith this way; One becoming fully persuaded that what God has promised, he is able to perform.

2. Hebrews 11:6 Without faith it is imposible to please him; for he that cometh to God must believe that he is, and that he is a rewarder of them that diligently seek him.

3. Romans 12:3b God has dealth to every man the measure of faith.

4. Romans 10:17 Faith cometh by hearing and hearing by the word of God.

5. 2 Corinthians 5:7 For we walk by faith, not by sight.

6. Galatians 5:6b Faith which worketh by love.

Now we will examine individuals who operated their faith properly and those who did not. We will also examine some other hindrance that can prevent one faith from operating properly or remaining strong. Lastly we will look at individuals who exercised great faith. We will look to see the characteristic traits of love that helped their faith to operate more effectively, because we understand according to Galatians 5:6b Faith worketh by love.

Now understand the indiviiduals we will examine are all under the old covenant. We now have a better covenant with better promises. (Hebrews 8:6) So we have an advantage the old testament believers didn't partake of. Understand, under the old covenant, the love of God was not shed abroad in the hearts of these believers. Only after Jesus ascended into heaven did the holy spirit indwell the hearts of believers during the day of Pentecost. But, these old covenant believers did understand they were loved by God with an everlasting love. (Jeremiah 31:3) And they understood they were to love their neighbors as themselves. (Leviticus 19:18)

ILLUSTRATIONS OF UNBELIEF

Now just as faith can accelerate a move of God, unbelief can stop or shut down a move of God. Let's define the word unbelief.

Unbelief- A lack of belief because of insufficient evidence

Remember faith needs no evidence according to (Hebrews 11:1).

Hebrews 3:19 So we see they could not enter in, because of unbelief

Amp. Ver. So we see that they were not able to enter in, because unbelief had shut them out.

There is a difference between doubt and unbelief.

Doubt- One is of 2 opinions, they doubt one minute and believe the next.

Unbelief- One remains with the same opinion consistently, they don't believe.

The first two stories will deal with unbelief. Mark 6:1-6 "Unbelief prevents Jesus from healing."

Now Jesus had been traveling from town to town, many signs, wonders and miracles had been following. Many were being healed, delivered and set free.

1. Now Jesus enters his own country, his disciples following him.

2. It is the Sabbath day; Jesus is the speaker for the service. The people are amazed at the wisdom he taught with and the power that flowed through him, they state; from whence hath this man these things?

3. So now they become offended with him, and state; Is not this the carpenter, the son of Mary, the brother of James, Joses, Juda and Simon? And are not his sisters here with us? Oh the sin of familiarity, it is now hindering them from receiving from Jesus.

    Understand these people had grown up with Jesus, they felt they were familiar with him. They felt they knew all about him. They were familiar with his Mom, his step Dad (Joseph) and his brothers and sisters, this was now hindering them from acknowledging the authority and power he now walked in.

4. Jesus responds, a prophet has honor except in his own country and amongst his kin and in his own house.

5. And because of the sin of familiarity, the people did not believe, and because they did not believe, Jesus couldn't do no mighty works except to heal a few sick people.

6. Jesus marvels because of their unbelief, and then he goes to teach in the surrounding villages.

    Understand Jesus was equipped with power, but unbelief shut down the move of God!

Our next story of unbelif comes from John 20:24-29 we will entitle this story," The unbelief of Thomas"

24 Our story begins with a man by the name of Thomas who is called Didymus, he was one of the twelve disciples of Jesus. Jesus had appeared to the other disciples, but Thomas was not present.

25 The other disciples said to Thomas, we have seen the Lord. Thomas responds, except I see in his hands the print of the nails, and put my finger into the nails, and thrust my hand into his side, I will not believe.

Understand unbelief is a choice, so is faith, Thomas is exercising his will here, he said I will or I chose not to believe. Thomas had a lot of variables he wanted to see before he believed. He refused to believe because of what he saw as a lack of evidence present. That's unbelief, when one chose not to belief because of what they see as insufficient evidence.

26 And after eight days pass; the disciples are all together, Thomas is with them, the doors are shut, Jesus appears, stands in their midst, and says peace be unto you.

27 Jesus then says unto Thomas, reach hither your finger and see my hands and put out your hand and place it in my side. Jesus says don't be faithless, but believing.

Remember God has given everyone the measure of faith,

(Roman12:3b) and he also honors faith. (Hebrews 11:6)

28 Thomas now answers and says, my Lord and my God.

Thomas now have evidence; he believes because of the evidence he can now see. Faith needs no evidence, just God's word. Faith is able to believe in spite of the lack of evidence present.

29 Jesus says unto Thomas, because you have seen me (you now have evidence) you have believed, blessed are those who have not seen me, and yet have believed. That's faith, faith need no evidence, just God's word! Romans 10:17

Jesus was teaching a lesson of faith. He said you are blessed if you can believe with no evidence present, that's faith and God honors faith (Hebrews 11:6) says; without faith it is impossible to please him.

More hindrances to one faith

We will look at some other hindrances that can prevent one faith from operating effectively.

Let's talk about one becoming impatient regarding Gods' promise.

Hebrews 6:12 That ye be not slothful but followers of them who through faith and patience inherit the promises.

Let's define the word patient,

Patient- One being able to wait calmly for something desired. (This, staying patient will help your faith) Let's now define the word impatient.

Impatient- Feeling or showing a lack of patience. Feeling or showing annoyance because of delay or opposition. (This, becoming impatient will hinder your faith)

Understand, one may be tempted to become impatient because their petition has not manifested, this will open the door to doubt, unbelief and fear. One need to understand faith and patience works together. Hebrews 6:12 says; That ye be not slothful but followers of them who through faith and patience inherit the promises.

David says, Psalms 40:1 I waited patiently for the Lord, and he inclined (attended) unto me and heard my cry. Understand the God who has made you the promise, will back up his word.

Numbers 23:19 states; God is not a man that he should lie, neither the son of man that he should repent, hath he said it, and shall he not do it, or hath he spoken and shall not make it good.

Luke 21: 19 says; In your patience (with your patience) possess ye your souls.

You take control of your soul (mind, will and emotions) you take charge of them.

Patience is a fruit of the spirit. Galatians 5:22 the fruit of longsuffering. The fruit of the spirit is imparted during our new birth, but it must be cultivated or developed.

How is patience developed? According to Romans 5:3b tribulation worketh (produces employs) patience. Understand, the devil is the one who brings tribulations, but God will use what the devil meant for evil to bring about the fruit of patience.

James 1:2-4 expounds how tribulation produces or employs patience.

> 2 My brethren count it all joy, when you fall into divers (different) temptations.

> 3 Knowing this that the trying (testing) of your faith worketh (produces employs) patience.

> 4 But let patience have her perfect (complete) work that ye may be perfect (completely developed in the fruit of patience) and entire wanting nothing.

Allow patience to run its' course (perfect work) that you can be completely developed in the fruit of patience. Now how does one know patience has had her complete work, ran its' course? When one can calmly wait on the promises of God! Remember Hebrews 6:12 That ye be not slothful but followers of them who through faith and patience inherit the promises.

If we would allow patience to be developed in us, our faith will work more effectively.

Illustrations of faith

Hebrews 11:2 For by faith the elders (men of old) obtained a good report. (we too can obtain a good report by faith)

Luke 18:35-43 "The blind man who received his sight"

35 Jesus comes near to Jericho. There is a blind man begging for alms by the roadside.

36 Although this man can't see, he hears the multitude passing by and then ask, what does it mean?

37 The people responded, Jesus of Nazareth is passing by.

38 He then cries out Jesus, thou son of David have mercy upon me.

Understand the blind mans' faith could have come by hearing testimonies about Jesus, he believed the word, meditated on the word he heard and now was ready to receive.

39 The people tried to quiet him down, but his faith is so built up, he cries out even more, thou son of David have mercy on me.

Understand this man faith is so built up, that the people can't shut him up! I say that's strong faith. He was fully persuaded that what God had promised, he was able to perform. Romans 4:21

40 Finally he gets Jesus attention, Jesus stops, he commanded the man to be brought to him.

God responds to faith, he rewards those who diligently seek him or seek him out (Hebrews 11:6)

41 Jesus now asked the man what is the need? He states; what wilt thou that I shall do unto thee? He responds, Lord that I may receive my sight.

Understand the blind man faith could have been, I believe Jesus is a healer, and if he ever comes to town, if I can just get an audience with him, I will be healed. We know this man faith was build up, and the people could not shut him up!

42 Jesus responds; receive your sight: your faith have saved you. (Amp. Version) your faith has healed you.

43 The blind man immediately receives his sight and follows Jesus glorifying God, which now causes the people to praise God as well.

Understand this man operated his faith properly, he didn't allow unbelief to hinder the move of God. We must believe God in spite of what people opinion of us maybe. The people around the blind man thought he should be quiet. God responds to faith, he sees the need and has promised to supply all of your needs (Philippians 4:19) but he expects you to exercise your faith to get the need met.

John 11:1-44 "The Resurrection of Lazarus" We will see in this story as Jesus performs this miracle, he requires those **around** him to stay in faith!

1 A man name Lazarus, who is from the town of Bethany is sick. He has 2 sisters, one name is Mary and the other Martha.

2 Mary, Lazarus' sister, had in past time anointed Jesus feet with ointment and wiped his feet with her hair.

3 Mary and Martha now sends word to Jesus, telling him, Lord, the one who you love (referring to Lazarus) is sick.

4 Jesus responds, this sickness is not unto death, but for the glory of God, that the son of God might be glorified.

Now here is a word from God, all who heard this word should have first believed it, and then begin to meditate upon those words. Remember faith comes or it is set in motion upon hearing a word from God (Romans 10:17) if we believe it!

Now one need to understand, God didn't make Lazarus sick in order that he may get glory, but God would rather use this sickness to bring him glory.

5 The story goes on to tell us, how Jesus loved Martha, Mary and Lazarus.

6 How-ever, when he gets word that Lazarus was sick, he remained in the same place for two more days.

Understand, Jesus didn't just drop everything and go to Lazarus, he rested in the spoken word that was given earlier, this sickness is not unto death but for the glory of God, that the son of God might be glorified.

7 Jesus then tells his disciples lets' go into Judea.

8 The disciples' responds, master the Jews recently were intending to try to stone you there, and will you go again?

9 Jesus answered, Are there not twelve hours in the day? If any man walks in the day, he does not stumble, because he sees the light of this world (Amp. Ver.) sees by the light of this world.

10 Jesus goes on to say; But if a man walks in the night, he will stumble, because there is no light in him. (Amp Ver.) the light is lacking to him.

11 Jesus then says, our friend Lazarus is sleep, but I'm going to awake him out of his sleep.

Understand Jesus said Lazarus is sleep, he believed the spoken word, this sickness is not unto death, but for the glory of God that the son of God might be glorified.

12 The disciples respond, Lord if he's asleep he shall do well.

13 This verse tells us, Jesus spoke of Lazarus' death, but the disciples didn't understand, they thought he meant Lazarus was sleep as in resting.

14 Jesus then plainly tells them, Lazarus is dead.

15 And he says, I'm glad for your sakes that I was not there, because now you will have an opportunity to believe. Jesus then tells them let's go unto him.

16 Thomas says unto the other disciples, let us go that we may die with him.

17 Jesus makes his arrival; he finds Lazarus has been dead in the grave for four days.

18 Our story goes on to say, Bethany was near Jerusalem about fifteen furlongs or two miles away.

19 Many of the Jews are with Mary and Martha comforting them.

20 Martha hears Jesus is coming and goes to meet him, while Mary remains in the house.

21 Martha meets Jesus, she says Lord, if you had been here my brother wouldn't have died.

22 She goes on to say, but I know, even now, whatever you ask God, God will give it unto you.

Martha apparently hadn't meditated upon the words spoken by Jesus earlier or perhaps she didn't fully understand them. Here is the spoken word given by Jesus, this sickness is not unto death, but for the glory of God, that the son of God might be glorified. Had she understood this word it should have been meditated upon until it was seeded in the heart and now it would have been coming out of her mouth! Matthew 12:34

23 Jesus responds your brother shall rise again. (Martha now has the spoken word again for the second time)

24 Martha respond; I know he will rise again in the resurrection at the last day. (she is now referring to the last days or the end of the age)

25 Jesus responds, I am the resurrection, and the life. He that believe in me, though he were dead yet shall he live.

26 He goes on to say; and whosoever liveth and believeth in me shall never die. He then ask Martha, Do you believe this?

27 Martha responds; Yes, Lord: I believe you are the Christ, (anointed Messiah) the son of God which should come into the world.

28 After Martha said this, she went and secretly tells Mary, the master is come and he is calling for you.

29 As soon as Mary heard the news, she arises quickly and goes to Jesus.

30 This verse tells us how Jesus hadn't come to town yet, but was still in the same place Martha had met him.

31 The Jews who were in the house with Mary comforting her, followed her when they saw she arose hastily, they were thinking she was going to the grave of her brother to weep.

32 Mary now meets Jesus, she falls at his feet and says the same thing her sister Martha said, she says, Lord if you had been here my brother wouldn't have died.

Now Mary heard the spoken word given by Jesus, she too hadn't meditated upon this word or perhaps she too didn't understand it. This sickness is not unto death, but for the glory of God, that the son of God might be glorified. If the word was properly meditated upon, it would have now been coming out of the mouth of Mary also.

33 Jesus sees Mary and the Jews with her crying, he then groans in the spirit and is troubled.

34 Jesus then ask, where have you laid him? They respond, Lord come and see.

35 Jesus weeps.

36 Some of the Jews responds, behold how he loved him.

37 But others said, could not this man who have opened blind eyes, prevented this man from dying?

38 Jesus again groans in himself and comes to the grave. Now the grave was a cave with a stone laid on it.

39 Jesus said, take away the stone, Martha responds, Lord by this time he stinketh, for Lazarus had been dead four days.

40 Jesus says to Martha, didn't I tell you, if you would believe you would see the glory of God?

Jesus is encouraging Martha to stay in faith, God honors faith, meditate on the spoken word given. Your brother shall rise again. This is what we must do when God has given us his word. There will always be circumstances that will arise that will look completely contrary to Gods' word. But remember one must use their faith even when the evidence can't be seen. We walk by faith, not by sight. (2 Corinthians 5:7)

41 The men now remove the stone, Jesus lifts up his eyes and prays, Father I thank you, that you have heard me.

42 And I know you hear me always, but for the sake of the people who are standing here, I said this that they may believe that you have sent me.

How could Jesus pray with such confidence? Jesus had a spoken word given by the Father earlier. This sickness is not unto death, but for the glory of God, that the son of God might be glorified. The word of God tells us in 1 John 5:14,15

14 And this is the confidence that we have in him, that if we ask anything according to his will, he heareth us.

15 And if we know that he hear us, whatsoever we ask, we know that we have the petitions that we desired of him.

Understand the word of God is the will of God! So Jesus knew he wasn't praying amiss, he was praying Gods' will, he had his word. Now understand it is not Gods' will to raise every dead person from their death bed, some have finished their course.

43 After Jesus had finished his prayer, he said with a loud voice, Lazarus, come forth!

Understand when we have God's word there is power, whether it is his written word or a spoken word. God used his powerful word to create the heavens and the earth. We need to understand the power that lies in the word of God.

44 The word of God says; And he that was dead came forth, bound hand and foot with his grave clothes on. His face bound with a napkin. Jesus said unto them, loose him and let him go. (Amp. Ver.) free him of the burial wrappings.

Understand when God word goes out of his mouth, it has an assignment. Isaiah 55:11 So shall my word that goeth forth out of my mouth, it shall not return unto me void, but it shall accomplish that which I please, and it shall prosper in the thing where to I sent it. When Jesus said come forth, Lazarus must have come forth.

Remember, whatever God has promise you, it must come forth, but you must believe it!

Let's look at our next story Matthew 8:28-32 "The devils believe and tremble"

Understand, the devil is our enemy, he seeks to steal Gods' word, because he is a thief. John 10:10 says; The thief cometh not, but for to steal, and to kill and to destroy. I am come that they may have life, and that they might have it more abundantly.

James 2:19 says; You believe that there is one God, you do well, the devils also believe, and tremble.

We may from time to time struggle to believe things God has spoken to us, but the word says, the devils believe and tremble. They understand the power that lies in Gods' word. We must have faith in Gods' word as well.

28 Jesus comes into the country of Gergesenes. He is met by two men possessed. (control by devils) The men are coming out of the tomb and they are exceeding fierce, (violent) that no one can pass by that way.

29 When the men see Jesus, the devils cry out, what have we to do with thee, Jesus thou son of God? are you come to torment us before the time?

Understand the devils understand the power (authority) of Gods' word!

30 The word says some herd of swine (pigs) were a distant away grazing. (eating)

31 The devils then plead with Jesus, if you cast us out, send us into the swine.

Gods' word is just that powerful, the devils believe it, but if the devil can convince you to doubt it, it will hinder your faith!

32 Jesus then speaks one word to them, he says go! The devils come out of the man and enters into the herd of swine, (pigs) and as a result of the devils entering into the pigs, the pigs run violently down a steep place and drowns into the sea.

That's the power that lies in Gods' word, we must believe it. It doesn't matter if it is the written word, or a spoken word. (prophetic word)

If its' authored by God, we must believe it.

It doesn't have to be a lot of words. One word from God can change a nation, that's' how powerful the word of God is. Believe it, meditate upon it. The devils believe and so must we!

Illustration of those who exercised great faith

Let's look at an example of a man that exercised great faith. Jesus complimented this man faith, he called it great! So we will examine his faith, we will also look for characteristics traits of love that help guard his faith, because we understand according to Galatians 5:6b Faith worketh by love.

Luke 7:1-10 "The healing of a centurion servant"

1 Jesus arrives in Capernaum.

2 Here's the problem, a centurion had a servant who was dear to him, he was sick and ready to die.

3 The centurion hears Jesus is in town. He sends elders of the Jews beseeching (begging) Jesus to come and heal his servant.

Understand his faith probably came (was set in motion) by hearing testimonies about Jesus.

4 The elders now begged Jesus to come, they proceed to tell Jesus why the man is worthy of his prayers.

5 They now begin to tell Jesus of the man's reputation, they state; that he loved the nation and have built them a synagogue.

6 Jesus agrees to come, he almost reaches his destination, but the centurion sends friends telling Jesus not to come, they state; Lord trouble not yourself. The centurion says, he doesn't feel worthy for Jesus to come under his roof.

7 He goes on to tells Jesus, neither did he feel worthy to come unto him, but he says; just say in a word or speak the word, and my servant will be healed.

8 The centurion proceeds to say, I am a man set under authority, having soldiers under me. I say unto one, Go and he goeth; and to another, Come, and he cometh; and to my servant, Do this and he doeth it.

Now this centurion was a man who was in authority. He too was a man also subject to authority. He had soldiers under him who carried out his orders, so this centurion well understood how authority operated. He understood how the chain of command worked. He knew Jesus was a man of authority, so he knew the power his word carried. He didn't need Jesus to come and lay hands on his servant nor did he need to touch the hem of his garment. He said speak the word only and his servant would be healed. He was fully persuaded what God had promised, he was able to perform. Romans 4:21

9 Jesus now marvels at the faith this man is exercising. He tells the people he hadn't found great faith like this, no-where in Israel, he calls the centurion faith, great faith.

10 The friends now return to the house of the centurion, and finds the servant who was at the point of death, now whole. (healed)

Understand, this centurion must have understood Gods' love, because he operated in great faith.

Now let's examine the characteristics traits of love found demonstrated by this centurion, because Jesus called his faith great and we understand according to Galatians5:6b Faith worketh by love. We stated; when one can have a healthy perspective of God's love, they understand we are loved by God (Jeremiah 31:3) and they understand we are to extend Gods' love toward our fellow man. (Leviticus 19:18)

I've chosen 3 characteristics traits of love

1. Love vaunteth not itself.

   Amp. Ver. Love is not boastful or vainglorious.

   Do we see this particular trait of love demonstrated by this centurion? Yes; This centurion was not a man who was boastful or vain-glorious, one who constantly bragged of his accomplishments. He could have boasted in his status as a centurion, for he was a man who had some authority. He could have boasted in the fact that at his word men moved, but this man never boasted in who he was, rather we see in Luke 7:6 He doesn't feel worthy of Jesus entering into his home.

2. Love is not puffed up.

   Amp. Ver. Love does not display itself haughtily. It is not conceited (arrogant and inflated with pride).

   Do we see this trait of love demonstrated by the centurion? Absolutely, we can clearly see this man did not display himself in a prideful way, he didn't have an attitude where he felt he was better than everyone else, he instead walked in a spirit of humility. In Luke 7:6-8 this man, the centurion expresses humility, although he had authority and people moved at his command, he was not boastful nor was he prideful, he expresses to Jesus his job description in verse 8, he says; there are soldiers under me and I say to this one go and he goeth and to another come and he cometh, and to my servant do this and he doeth it. So we see he was not puffed up or we can say prideful.

3. Love does not behave itself unseemly.

    Amp. Ver. Love is not rude (unmannerly and does not act unbecomingly.

    Can we find this particular trait of love demonstrated by the centurion? Certainly, this man didn't behave himself unseemly (rude) we are able to see this by his very actions. He respected Jesus, held him in high regards. He even had high regards for his servant. Verse 2 says; his servant was very dear to him. This helps us to understand the heart of this centurion. He could have fired his servant when he fell ill. His attitude could have been his servant was no longer valuable to him now that he was sick, but we see this was not his attitude, instead he was seeking healing for his servant. He loved his neighbor as himself. (Leviticus 19:18)

    Now there is not a lot of information given about this centurion, but from everything we do have, we have to believe this centurion was a man who understood he was loved by God (Jeremiah 31:3) and he understood how to extend Gods' love toward his fellow man. (Leviticus 19:18) Now I need you to understand this, we are now living under a better covenant, with better promises (Hebrews 8:6) we are under grace! We have been made righteous by the blood Jesus shed on the cross. Now although God does require us to clothe our-selves in humility, (1 Peter 5:5b) we don't have to feel unworthy of God's presence like the centurion felt. Hebrews 4:16 says; Let's us come boldly unto the throne of grace, that we may obtain mercy and find grace to help in the time of need. We can come boldly into God's presence without any feelings of unworthiness. If we sin (miss the mark) we can repent and God is faithful and just to forgive us of our sins and to cleanse us from all unrighteousness. (1 JOHN 1:9)

    So we see the centurion faith was protected by the love he understood, because faith worketh by love. (Galatians 5:6b)

Lesson 3

Now let's review our 6 scritptures that speaks of faith

1. Romans 4:13,20,21

    13 For the promise, that he should be the heir of the world, was not to Abraham, or to his seed, through the law, but through the righteousness of faith.

    20 He (Abraham) staggered not at the promises of God through unbelief; but was strong in faith, giving glory to God;

    21 And being fully persuaded that, what he had promised, he was able also to perform.

    We define faith this way; One becoming fully persuaded that what God has promised, he is able also to perform.

2. Hebrews 11:6 Without faith it is impossible to please him, for he that cometh to God must believe that he is, and that he is a rewarder of them that diligently seek him.

3. Romans 12:3b God has dealt to every man the measure of faith.

4. Romans 10:17 Faith cometh by hearing and hearing by the word of God.

5.   2 Corinthians 5:17 For we walk by faith, not by sight.

6.   Galatians 5;6b Faith which worketh by love.

Now we will examine individuals who operated their faith properly and those who did not. We will also examine some other hindrance that can prevent one faith from operating properly or remaining strong. Lastly we will look at individuals who exercised great faith. We will look to see the characteristic traits of love that helped their faith to operate more effectively, because we understand according to Galatians 5:6b Faith worketh by love.

Now understand the individuals we will examine are all under the old covenant. We now have a better covenant with better promises. (Hebrews 8:6) So we have advantage the old testament believers didn't partake of. Understand, under the old covenant, the love of God was not yet shed aboard in the hearts of these believers. Only after Jesus ascended into heaven did the holy spirit indwell the hearts of believers during the day of Pentecost. But, these old covenant believers did understand they were loved by God with an everlasting love, (Jeremiah 31:3) And they understood they were to love their neighbors as themselves, (Leviticus 19:18)

Illustrations of unbelief

Now just as faith can accelerate a move of God, unbelief can stop or shut down a move of God. Let's define the word unbelief.

Unbelief- A lack of belief because of insufficient evidence.

Understand faith needs no evidence, it believes in spite of evidence. (Hebrews 11:1)

There is a difference between doubt and unbelief.

Doubt- One is of two opinions, they believe one minute and doubt the next.

Unbelief- One remains of the same opinion consistently, they don't believe.

Hebrews 3:19 So we see they could not enter in because of unbelief.

Amp. Ver. So we see that they were not able to enter in, because unbelief had shut them out.

Luke 1:5-20, Luke 1: 61-64

"The unbelief of Zacharias"

5 Our story begins with a man by the name of Zacharias, he was a priest and from the division of Abia. He had a wife by the name of Elizabeth.

6 The word of God says, they were both righteous and were following Gods' commandments and ordinances. The word calls them blameless.

7 The word tells us, they had no children, because Zacharias wife Elizabeth was barren, and now both of them are well stricken or far advanced in years.

8 Mean-while Zacharias is executing the duty of the priest in the order of his division.

9 Now according to custom of the priesthood, it fell to Zacharias by lot to burn incense, so he entered the temple to do so.

10 Now there was a multitude of people praying outside of the court at the hour of incense burning.

11 An angel of the Lord appears unto Zacharias; he stands on the right side of the altar.

12 Zacharias sees the angel, he becomes troubled and fear falls upon him.

13 The angel tells Zacharias to fear not, for his prayers have been heard. He says, your wife Elizabeth will have a son and you are to name him John.

14 The angel goes on to tell Zacharias, the child will bring joy and gladness and many other people will rejoice at his birth.

Now here is a word from the Lord spoken to Zacharias. Now Zacharis should have believed that word and then begin to meditate the word spoken. But let's continue our story.

15 The angel continues to give Zacharias further instructions about the child's destiny. He tells him the child will be greatly used by God, and he will not drink wine or strong drink, he says that he will be filled with the holy-ghost from his mother's womb.

16 The angel says many of the children of Israel will God use the child to turn their hearts toward the Lord their God.

17 He continues to say, the child John will be used like Elijah, he will turn the hearts of the Fathers' to the children and the disobedient to the wisdom of the just and he will make ready a people prepared for the Lord.

18 Zacharias now responds, he says, where by or how shall I know this? He says he is an old man and his wife Elizabeth is well stricken (well advanced) in years.

Now here is unbelief, Zacharias refuses to believe because of the ages of he and his wife. He felt they were both too old. He should have exercised his faith here, believe Gods' word meditate upon it, and then left all the variables he didn't understand unto God. His meditation should have been, I will have a son and his name will be called John.

19 The angel Gabriel now rebukes Zacharias, he reminds him who brought the word, he says I am Gabriel and I stand in Gods' presence. I have been sent by God to speak unto you, to bring you glad tidings or (good news).

Understand when God speaks a word to us, it should be a time of celebration, even before we see the manifestation.

20 The angel now tells Zacharias, he will be dumb, not able to speak, until the day that these words are performed, because he didn't believe, how-ever; God said the word spoken would be fulfilled in its' season.

One must understand, God is a God that requires faith. Hebrews 11:6 says; Without faith it is impossible to please him. So now God closes the mouth of Zacharias, so he wouldn't shut down the move of God with his doubt and unbelief. The story goes on to say that Elizabeth does becomes pregnant and brings forth the child and names him John. Let's continue our story beginning at verse 61.

61 Now Elizabeth neighbors and cousins wants Elizabeth to name the child after Zacharias, his Dad, they say no one of his kin name is John.

62 They then begin to make signs to Zacharias, trying to find out what he wanted the child to be called.

63 Zacharias now ask for a writing tablet, he writes, the child name is John. They all marvel.

64 The word says, immediately Zacharias mouth was opened and his tongue is loosed and he begins to speak and praise God.

Understand the manifestation has arrived, Zacharias unbelief was not able to hinder the move of God.

Zacharias should have had the same attitude that Abraham had, he was not the first person God had required this from. He required the same thing from Abraham and Sarah, they too were both well stricken in age when God promised them a son. Let's examine Abraham's attitude. The word of God says this about Abrahams' faith.

Romans 4:19-21

19 Abraham being not weak in faith. He considered not his own body now dead, when he was about a hundred years old. Neither yet the deadness of Sarah's womb (Sarah was 90 years old)

20 He staggered (doubted) not at the promise of God through unbelief; but was strong in faith, giving glory to God.

21 And being fully persuaded that, what God had promised, he was able also to perform.

Understand the word of the Lord should bring a celebration even before the manifestation. Abraham left all the variables he may not have understood unto God. He chose to believe the word of the Lord. This should have been the attitude of Zacharias in spite of the ages of he and Elizabeth. The word of the Lord should bring a celebration (praise) even before the manifestation is seen. Now Sarah, Abraham's wife did try to help God to bring about the fulfillment of the promise. (Genesis 16:1,2) nevertheless, although Abraham cooperated will Sarah's plan, when God approach him once more regarding the promise, Abraham chose to believe God once again. We will study more about the faith of Abraham later on in our lesson.

More hindrances to one faith

Let's talk about faith with no corresponding actions to go alone with it.

James 2:20b Faith without works is dead.

Now here is something one needs to understand about one faith according to 1Corinthians 12:4-6 It states,

4 Now there are diversities of gifts, but the same spirit.

5 And there are differences of administration's or different kinds of services (New International Version) but the same lord.

6 And there are diversities of operations, but it is the same God which worketh all in all.

Now faith is a gift that can service one in many different ways. It will service any believer salvation, according to Romans 10:9

Understand no amount of works done by the believer could ever earn them their salvation. It is a gift from God. Ephesians 2:8,9

Understand the work has been completed by Jesus when he died on the cross. However, faith will also service any believer the aid to getting their needs met according to Mark 9:23 It states, If thou can't believe all things are possible to him that believe.

Now this service of faith that will aid believer's in getting their needs met, may sometimes require more works on the believer's part.

Let's look at an example where the kind of faith that enables the believer needs to be met, would require works. Let's say some one is believing God to receive a job, well this will require works on the part of this believer, you stay in faith, but you also for the most part will have to begin to look for that job. So, with that understanding, let's talk about faith with no corresponding action is dead.

James 2: 14—26

14 James states; What doth it profit, my brethren, though a man say he hath faith, and have not works? Can faith save him?

15 He now gives us an example of faith with no works, he says; If a brother or sister is naked and have no daily food,

16 And one of you say unto them, Depart in peace, be warmed and filled, but you don't give him clothes or food (have no works accompanying) he says; what have you profit?

17 He goes on to say; Even faith, if it has no works, it is dead, being alone.

18 James says; If a man says you have faith and I have works, he then says show me your faith, without your works, and I will show you my faith by my works.

19 He then states; You believe there is one God, you do well, he says the devils believe, and tremble.

20 He then calls a person vain (empty of no value) who has faith but no works (accompanying, following) their faith, he says; But wilt thou know, O vain man, that faith without works is dead?

21 James now uses Abraham as an example, he says; Was not Abraham our Father justified (acceptable to God) because of his works, when he offered up Isaac his son upon the altar?

22 He says, do you see how his faith cooperated with his works, and by his works was faith made perfect? (complete)

23 James says; And the scripture was fulfilled which says, Abraham believed (had faith) in God, and it was imputed (credited) unto him for righteousness: and he was called the friend of God.

24 He says; You now see how that by works a man is justified, and not faith only.

25 He now gives the example of Rehab (harlot, prostitute) how God honored her because of her works. He says; Likewise also was not Rehab the harlot justified by works, when she received the messengers, and had sent them out another way?

26 He then concludes by stating; For as the body without the spirit is dead, so faith that has no works (accompanying, following) it, is dead.

Your works should demonstrate your faith, and your faith should produce works!

Illustrations of faith

Hebrews 11:2 For by faith the elders (men of old) obtained a good report. (we too can obtain a good report by faith)

Genesis 22:1-14 "Abraham's faith confirmed' Now this story is coming from the old testament. We are now living under a new covenant, Romans 15:4 tells us; For whatsoever things were written afore time, (before) time, were written for our learning. So understand, we can learn lessons from the old testament and apply them to our lives today. But I also want you to understand, we are no longer under the law, so we no longer use burnt offerings as we will read about in this story. Jesus became the perfect sacrifice when he gave his life. So with that understanding let's begin!

1 Our story begins with God testing Abraham's faith, God calls out to Abraham, Abraham responds, here am I.

2 God tells Abraham to take his only son Isaac whom he loves, and go to the land of Moriah, and offer up Isaac there for a burnt offering. God then instructs Abraham about a mountain, he says the mountain I will tell you about.

3 The word tells us; Abraham rises up early in the morning, saddles his donkey, and takes two of his young men with him, along with his son Isaac. He splits the wood for the burnt offering, rises up, and begins his journey to the place God instructs.

4 Abraham continues his journey for three days. He then looks up and sees the place at a far distance.

5 Abraham now instructs the young men, to stay with the donkey; while he and his son Isaac go yonder and worship and return to them again.

Let's examine Abraham's faith here, God had told Abraham to kill his son Isaac. Abraham faith was, if he kills his son, then God would have to raise him up again. How could Abraham have so much confidence here? God had given Abraham a word regarding Isaac destiny. Genesis 17:9 God told Abraham he would establish a covenant with Isaac his seed after him. Abraham had believed that word, meditated the word, it was now in his heart coming out of his mouth. Matthew 12:34

6 Abraham now takes the wood for the burnt offering, lays it upon Isaac shoulder, he takes the fire or (fire pan) in his hand along with his knife and he and Isaac leaves together.

7 Isaac then says to Abraham, my Father, Abraham responds; Here am I my son. Isaac says behold here is the fire and the wood, but where is the lamb for the burnt offering?

8 Abraham tells Isaac, my son, God will provide himself a lamb for the burnt offering. So they continue their journey.

9 Mean-while, they now arrive at the appointed place, appointed by God. Abraham builds there an altar. He lays the wood in place, bound (ties) Isaac his son, and lays him on the altar on the wood.

10 Abraham now stretches forth his hand, takes the knife and is ready to kill Isaac.

11 The angel of the Lord calls out to Abraham from heaven, he says Abraham, Abraham, Abraham respond; Here am I.

12 The angel then tells him, don't lay your hands upon the child, don't do anything unto him, for he says; now I know you fear (revere, honor, respect) God because you did not with-hold your son, your only son from me.

Understand God knew that Abraham feared (reverence) him by his works. (James 2:18b) Says, I will show you my faith by my works.

13 Abraham now lifts up his eyes, and sees behind him a ram caught in the thickets (small trees or shrub) he takes him by his horn, Abraham now offers the ram up for a burnt offering instead of his son Isaac.

14 Abraham then calls the name of that place Jehovah- jireh, (The Lord my provider) for it is said to this day, In the mount of the Lord it shall be seen.

Understand, Abraham was a man of faith and his works demonstrated his faith!

Let's examine our next story. We will look at a man who had a son that was possessed by a demon. This man was so over-whelmed by his situation, he couldn't operate his faith properly, so Jesus stepped in and used his faith.

Mark 9:17-23 "Jesus cast out a dumb spirit"

17 Our story begins with a man who brings to Jesus his son that has a dumb spirit.

18 The man goes on to tell Jesus of the boy's condition, he says; when-ever the spirit takes control of him, it throws him down, and convulses him, he foams (at the mouth) and grinds his teeth, and then pineth away. (Is wasting away) He then tells Jesus, that he had asked the disciples to cast the spirit out of the boy, but they could not.

19 Jesus then responds, he says O faithless generation, how long shall I be with you? How long shall I suffer you? He tells the man to bring the boy unto him.

Understand Jesus didn't say powerless generation, but faithless generation. It was a faith issue that hinder the disciples from helping the boy.

20 The people brings the child to Jesus, when the spirit sees Jesus, the child has a convulsion, (seizure) he falls to the ground and begins to wallow on the ground and foam at the mouth.

21 Jesus then ask the Father, how long has this been going on? The man says since he was a child.

22 The man goes on to tell Jesus what the spirit has done to try to destroy the child in time-past. He says; many times it has cast him into the fire and into water to destroy him: he says to Jesus, if you can do anything have compassion on us and help us.

23 Jesus then says to the man, If you can believe (have faith) all things are possible to him that believeth.

Now Jesus could have cast the spirit out immediately, but he wanted the man to understand, his faith if exercised properly was capable of getting the job done!

24 The man immediately cries out to Jesus with tears, he says; Lord I believe, but help my unbelief.

In other-words the man is saying, I'm trying to believe, but doubt keeps entering into the picture. This man had probably seen so much it was now challenging his faith. He was trying to exercise his faith, but doubt kept entering the picture. Jesus now takes control exercising his faith.

25 Jesus now notice the crowd of people (running) together, he rebukes the foul (unclean spirit) he says; you dumb and deaf spirit I charge you (command you) to come out of him, and enter no more into him.

26 The spirit then rent him sore (terribly) and then it comes out of him. The boy then lays motionless as if he is dead, so much that many thought he was dead.

27 But Jesus now takes the boy by the hand and lifts him up and the boy arises. (stands up)

28 Jesus and his disciples now leaves and enters into a house, the disciples ask Jesus a question, they ask why couldn't we cast out the spirit?

29 Jesus then says, this kind can't be driven out but by prayer and fasting.

The disciple's problem wasn't that they didn't have the power, but the absence of faith, doubt was the issue. The disciples had gone out previously and had gotten positive results using their authority. An example of this is found in Mark 6:13 Jesus sends his disciples out two by two and gave them power over unclean spirits. The word says and they (disciples) cast out many devils and anointed with oil many that were sick, and healed them.

So we see power wasn't the issue that prevented them from helping the boy, it was a lack of faith. (doubt) The demon possessed child was now a challenge to their faith (2 Corinthians 5:7) says we walk by faith, not by sight. Unbelief had to be defeated and Jesus encouraged them to do this, they needed to pray and fast.

Illustration of those who exercised great faith

2 Kings 4:16-37 "The faith of the Shunammite Woman and Elisha"

Now this Shunammite woman is known as a woman of faith. She is mentioned in the hall of faith. (Hebrews 11:35) She was known to have great faith, so we will now read the story, and then examine some characteristics traits of love that help to protect her faith. Because we understand according to Galatians 5:6b faith works by love, when one has a healthy perspective of God's love. Understand, these old covenant believers, did not have the love of God shed abroad in their hearts by the holy ghost, because the holy spirit had not yet come in the earth to dwell in the hearts of all believers. But, they understood they were loved by God (Jeremiah 31:3) and they understood they had been given a charge to extend the love of God toward their fellow man. (Leviticus 19:18)

> 16 Elisha prophesies to the Shunammite woman, here is the word of the Lord, he says you will have a son at this season according unto the time of life. (next year) The woman responds, No, my Lord, you man of God, don't lie unto your hand maid.

> Now this woman's faith was in God, but also in the prophet Elisha. She believed Elisha was a man of God who spoke on God's behalf. Let's now continue to examine this woman's faith.

> 17 The woman conceives just as the word of the Lord says, and brings forth a son.

46

18 The child is grown, and goes out to his Father with the reapers into the field.

19 The child complains about his head unto his Father, his Father tells a lad to take him unto his Mother.

20 The child is taken to his Mother, sits on her knees until noon and then dies.

21 The woman takes the dead child, lays him on the bed of the man of God, closes the door upon him and leaves.

Now let's follow this woman's faith, she now exercises her faith as far as she can believe, and the man of God, Elisha, then uses his faith.

22 She then tells her husband, send one of the servant and a donkey, that she needed to go unto the man of God quickly.

23 Her husband responds, why go to the man of God? it's not the new moon nor the Sabbath. (not a special holy day) she responds, it shall be well.

Let's examine her faith thus far, she didn't explain why she needed to go to the man of God. She only reply, it shall be well. This woman was guarding her faith. She took no chances on explaining herself. She didn't want doubt, unbelief, or fear to enter the picture.

24 She now saddles the donkey, then instructs the servant to drive and go forward, don't slack your driving for no one except I tell you to do so.

This woman is still guarding her faith, she understands interactions here would not be good, there might have been the possibility of the subject coming up, how is your son?

25 She makes her arrival to Mount Carmel where the man of God is. Elisha spots her afar off. He points her out to his servant Gehazi, he says; Behold, yonder is that Shunammite.

26 He tells his servant Gehazi, run to go meet her, ask her is it well with her? is it well with her husband? is it well with the child? She now responds; It is well.

Now notice her words are altered a bit, she started off by telling her husband, it shall be well, but now when she sees Elisha, she says it is well. Her faith must have been, if I could just get to the man of God who spoke the word of the Lord, all will be well. So this must have been her meditation all the way there.

27 She finally meets Elisha, she grabs his feet, Gehazi attempts to stop her, but Elisha tells him to leave her alone, he senses something is wrong because she is vexed in her soul, but he is not quite sure just what the problem is, because God has not yet revealed this unto him.

28 She now speaks; she says to Elisha, did I not desire a son of my Lord? Did I not say, Do not deceive me?

This woman faith took her to her destination, her faith was guarded, protected from doubt, unbelief and fear but this is as far as she can exercise her faith. She is now relying on Elisha to exercise his faith, after all he was the one who had spoken the word of the Lord to her regarding her son.

29 Elisha being in tune with God's spirit, needed no further words. He now instructs his servant Gehazi to gird up your loins and take my staff, he says; If you meet any man, don't salute him; and if he salute you, don't answer him. He then instructs him to lay his staff upon the face of the child.

Now Elisha is doing the same thing the Shunammite woman did, he's guarding the faith. He forbids his servant to talk to no-one. Doubt, unbelief or fear might enter the picture. Understand one has to be careful some-times about speaking God's promises prematurely, everyone may not believe, and God honors faith!

30 The Shunammite tells Elisha, as the Lord liveth and as your soul liveth, I won't leave you, Elisha arise and follows her.

Now this Shunammite woman is relying on the faith of Elisha to operate, she has taken her faith as far as she can believe.

31 Gehazi does exactly what he was told to do by Elisha, he lays Elisha's staff upon the face of the child, but there is still no sign of life. He reports back to Elisha; he says the child is not awake.

Now notice how all parties are guarding their faith, no-one speaks of the death of the child.

32 Elisha goes to the house, the word let us know the child is dead upon Elishas' bed.

33 Elisha goes into the house, he closes the door and begins to pray. He gets the mind of the God just what to do

34 He then lays upon the child, put his mouth upon his mouth, his eyes upon his eyes, his hands upon his hands and stretches himself upon the child, the child now waxes (becomes) warm.

Understand, this is the first sign of life. Everything up to this point was faith in operation.

35 This verse tells us Elisha returns again, he walks to and fro in the house. He then stretches himself upon the child once again, the child now sneezes seven times, (representing completion) he then opens his eyes.

36 Elisha calls Gehazi his servant, he tells him to call the Shunammite woman. Gehazi calls her, Elisha tells the woman to take up her son.

Her son is now the manifestation of her faith and the prophet Elisha. The evidence can now be seen.

37 The Shunammite woman now falls at Elisha feet, bows herself to the ground and takes up her son and leaves.

Now let's examine the characteristics traits of love that was demonstrated by this Shunammite woman. Because we understand faith worketh by love (Galatians 5:6b) When one has a healthy understanding of God's love. They understand they are loved by God (Jeremiah 31:3) and have a charge to extend the love of God toward their fellow man. (Leviticus 19:18)

I have chosen 3 characteristics traits of love.

Understand this woman must have understood she was loved by God and therefore she was able to extend Gods' love toward her fellowman. Had this Shunammite woman not understood God's love for her, she may have not being able to trust God.

1. Love doeth not behave itself unseemly.

   Amp. Ver. Love is not rude. (unmannerly and does not act unbecomingly)

   Can we find this trait of love demonstrated by this Shunammite woman? Certainly, this woman was presented with many opportunities to act unseemly or rude. She was under great distress; she had just lost her son. This would have been challenging for any one faith, but this woman still exhibited love.

   Now this woman had interactions with 4 people during her painful ordeal. Let's examine her behavior.

   2 Kings 4:16-37

   The 1st encounter was with her husband. When life left her child, she sends word to her husband in verse 22 she tells him to send one of the servants and a donkey, that she needed to go to the man of God quickly.

   Verse 23 Tells us her husband responds, why do you need to go to the man of God, it's neither new moon or the Sabbath. She only responds, it shall be well. Now here was an opportunity where she could have been rude or fearful, she could have responded, stop all these questions, just send me the servant and the donkey! But her faith is protected from fear, doubt and unbelief by the love she understood. She continues to trust God and to extend Gods' love toward her fellowman.

The 2nd encounter was with her servant the driver in verse 24 She now gives him clear instructions, they were he was to drive and don't stop for anyone accept she tells him to. There are no other words recorded that was exchanged between the two of them. Understand this man was her servant, he worked for her, she could have become fearful and very irritable toward him, but she continues to trust God and to extend the love of God toward her fellowman.

The 3rd encounter is with the servant of Elisha, Gehazi, in verse 26 Elisha spots this woman from a distant, he sends his servant Gehazi to inquire was everything ok with everyone; She responds; It is well, once again here's an opportunity for her to become rude, fearful, filled with doubt and unbelief. She was coming to speak with Elisha and instead she's met by his servant. Now she could have said, I don't want to speak to you, just take me to your master, but she continues to demonstrate the love of God.

Finally, the 4th encounter, she meets Elisha, in verse 27 she now grabs him by the feet, she then reminds him of the words she had spoken after he had given her the word of the Lord. verse 28, she says, did I desire a son of my Lord? Did I not say do not deceive me? Once again here is an opportunity she could have gotten rude, became fearful, filled with doubt and unbelief, she could have called Elisha a liar, a deceiver, but she continues to keep herself in the love of God. She continues to trust God, understanding his love for her.

This woman understood she was loved by God and she walked in the love of God toward her fellow man.

2. Love is not easily provoked.

Amp. Ver. Love is not touchy or fretful or resentful.

Do we see this trait of love demonstrated by this Shunammite woman? Yes, one can clearly see this woman wasn't easily provoked (upset), she wasn't touchy, fretful or resentful. Once again we will examine the 4 encounters this woman experienced during her ordeal.

In verse 22, her 1st encounter, she informed her husband she was going to the man of God, and he asked why, her response was it shall be well.

Now notice she was not touchy fretful or resentful toward her husband, she could have accused him of being responsible for their son accident, but she didn't. We can see this woman trusted God and she was able to extend Gods' love toward her fellowman.

In verse 24, her 2nd encounter, now she interacts with her driver, her words to him were to drive and don't stop for anyone accept I tell you. Here her words are firm but not harsh, no sign of her being easily provoked nor were she fretful. Her faith is continued to be protected by love. She trusted God that she would receive a miracle.

In verse 26, her 3rd encounter, she now interacts with Elisha servant Gehazi. When she arrives she is met by him although she had come to see Elisha (his master). Gehazi ask is everything well with everyone? she responds, all is well, we see no sign she is provoked with anger nor is she touchy or even fretful by his servant question. We also see her response was not made with provoking words such as, just get me your master, stop wasting my time. She continues to trust God.

And finally in verse 28, her 4th encounter, she's met by Elisha the man of God, now although she becomes emotional here, she grabs his feet, but the words she speaks are not provoking. She reminds him of the words she had spoken when he had given her the word of the Lord, she says, did I not desire a son? did I not say do not deceive me? Although she is emotional here, she continues to protect her faith, she keeps her-self in the love of God instead of accusing Elisha.

3. Love believeth all things.

    Amp. Ver. Love is ever ready to believe the best of every person.

    Do we see this trait of love demonstrated by this Shunammite woman? Certainly,

    We see this Shunammite woman kept a positive attitude toward Elisha and God. She chose to believe the best of them both. The devil is the accuser of the brethren, I'm sure he tried accusing Elisha and God of failing her, but she made the choice to believe the best in spite of what the evidence appeared to look like.

So understand, this woman faith was protected by the love she understood God had for her. She exercises her faith to the extent she could believe. Her faith was, God would use Elisha the man of God, who had spoken the word of the Lord, to raise her son up from his death bed. She guarded her faith until she reached the man of God. Elisha then exercised his faith and she received her miracle!

We too as believers must keep ourselves in the love of God. (Jude:21a) Know you are loved by God in spite of your failures and practice walking in the love of God toward your fellow man, because according to Galatians 5:6b Faith worketh by love!

Lesson 4

WHOLENESS FOR
THE TOTAL YOU

We are a triune (3 part being) We are spirit, soul and body. We are spirits that have souls that live in bodies. It's God desire that we are whole in each of these areas.

Paul says; 1Thessalonians 5:23 And the very God of peace sanctify you wholly (complete in every part, perfectly sound) and I pray your whole spirit and soul and body be preserved blameless unto the coming of our Lord Jesus Christ.

Understand you are not whole if your spirit alone is whole or if your soul and body alone is whole. God desires the totality of our being whole spirit, soul and body.

Let's talk briefly about each part of our being.

The spirit man- First one need to understand, we are really spirit beings. Our spirits will live eternally. We determine where our spirits will spend eternity by the decisions we make while we are in the earth, whether one chose to accept Jesus in their lives. Now the spirit enables one to fellowship with

God. When one spirit becomes born again, it then becomes alive unto God.

John 6:63 says; It is the spirit that quickeneth (comes alive) the flesh profiteth nothing, the words that I speak unto you, they are spirit and life.

The spirit gives life, the flesh or physical part has no life of its' own, its' totally dependent on the spirit life. When we talk to God, God also desires to talk with us, he desires fellowship. One of the ways God speaks to us is through our spirit man. One spirit should be born again, so it can become alive unto God.

For one spirit to become born again, one must according to Romans 10:9,10

> 9 One must confess with their mouth the Lord Jesus and believe in their hearts that God has raised Jesus from the dead, thou shalt be saved.

> 10 For with the heart man believe unto righteousness and with the mouth confession is made unto salvation.

> One should also seek to become filled with God's spirit as well.(Acts 1:8)

So this is your spirit, but we are spirit, soul and body, let's now identify the soul and the body.

The Soul- The soul is where one mind will and emotions resides, decision are made here, it is where one thought life lives.

The Body- The body is our physical house. It houses the spirit and the soul. This is how we identify one another, by our physical attributes. We ask questions like, how tall are they? What is their weight? What skin complexion are they? When we ask questions like these, we are referring to our physical attributes.

Now these are the 3 elements that makes up our being, the spirit, soul and body. We will examine how to become whole in each of these areas. Now understand, our being is made up of 3 parts spirit, soul and body, and each of these 3 elements has 3 parts that make them up as well. So let's first begin by talking about what makes up the spirit man.

The Spirit make up consist of 3 elements, they are: Intuition, Communion and Conscience.

Let's talk for a moment about each of these 3 elements that makes up the spirit man.

The first element of the spirit man is,
Intuition- This is the part of your spirit that some may refer to as your knower, you know things intuitively, you have this perception, that you are aware of things without the conscience use reasoning.

1 Corinthians 2:11 For what man knoweth the things of a man, save the spirit of man which is in him, even so the things of God knoweth no man, but the spirit of God.

The second element of the spirit man is,
Communion- This is the part of your spirit that longs to commune to fellowship with God.

Everyone has a place in them that longs to fellowship with God. It is a God spot that only God can fill. Now some maybe unaware of this and try to fill this spot by other means and still find no satisfaction.

Revelation 3:20 John records Jesus sayings, Behold I stand at the door and knock, if any man hear my voice and open the door, I will come in to him and sup (dine fellowship) with him and he with me.

The third element of the spirit man is,
Conscience- This is the part of your spirit that has an awareness of what is right and wrong.

John 8:9 And they which heard it, being convicted by their own conscience went out one by one beginning at the eldest even unto the last and Jesus was left alone and the woman standing in the midst.

This story is about a woman who was taken in the act of adultery, she was brought to Jesus by the scribes and Pharisee, they wanted to see Jesus' reaction, Jesus responded by saying, he that is without sin, let him cast the first stone.

There was no need for any further conversation, the word says they were convicted by their own conscience. They knew what was right and what was wrong.

So these are the 3 Elements our spirit, Intuition, Communion and Conscience.

Let's now talk about how to become strong (whole) in your spirit, because if you want to carry out exploits in the earth you want to be strong in each of these areas, spirit soul and body.

Daniel 11:32b But the people that do know their God shall be strong, and do exploits. (notable heroic acts)

Once the spirit becomes born again, one is now in an infancy stage spiritually. They are known as babies in Christ.

Luke 2:40 says, And the child (Jesus) grew, and waxed (became) strong in spirit, filled with wisdom and the grace of God was upon him.

So how does one become strong in spirit?

There are 3 components involved,

1. One should unite with a local church where there is sound teaching (ask guidance from the holy-spirit) and attend on a regular base.

    Hebrews 10:25 Not forsaking the assembling of ourselves as the manner of some, but exhorting one another and so much more as you see the day approaching.

2. One should study the word on a regular base.

   1 Peter 2:2 As new born babies, desire the sincere milk of the word, that ye may grow there by.

   The word will help you grow up, mature spiritually.

3. One should have a prayer life, pray on a regular base.

   Luke 18:1 Men ought always to pray and not to faint.

   Matthew 26:41 Jesus says, Watch and pray, that ye enter not into temptation, the spirit indeed is willing, but the flesh is weak.

   If you don't want to faint (weaken) learn to pray. The flesh doesn't want to pray, but the spirit is ready. (willing)

   Now if one studies the 4 gospel. Matthew, Mark, Luke and John, one will see Jesus used these 3 components to help develop his disciples. They came to him in the stage of infancy. He had 3 years with them and he brought them to a place of maturity.

   We see Jesus consistently gathering his disciples together, and when they came together he spent time teaching them the word and about prayer. So Jesus didn't forsake to assemble himself with his disciples.

   In Matthew 13:51 Jesus is found teaching his disciples and a multitude of people. He taught them in parables. After he had finished teaching he took his disciple apart from the multitude. He then explained the parables and asked his disciples, have ye understood all these things? Jesus made sure his disciples had a good understanding of the word.

   Jesus also took time to teach his disciples how to pray. Luke 11:1 One of his disciples asked him, Lord teach us to pray as John also taught his disciples. Jesus then taught them what is known as the Lord's prayer.

So this is how one spirit becomes strong, by the use of these 3 components,

A Not forsaking to assemble yourselves with other believers.

Hebrews 10:25

B The studying of the word 1 Peter 2:2

C Prayer Luke 18:1

A strong diet of the word and prayer is very necessary for your development of a strong spirit. One should do your personal study of the word and have personal prayer time, along with attending bible study and prayer meetings at your local assemble. Understand consistency is very important, because you don't want to stop short of becoming whole, but also remaining whole and to remain whole one must apply consistency.

Now let's talk about the soul, remember we want to be whole spirit, soul and body!

Now the soul is some-what more complex. Everything, spirit and body relies on the soul prospering. 3 John:2-Beloved, I wish above all things that thou prosper and be in health, even as thy soul prospereth.

The soul make- up consist of 3 elements as well, they are, the mind, will and emotions.

The first element that makes up the soul is the mind.

The mind is the part of our soul where our thought life resides. It's where thoughts are meditated upon. We understand from God's word that it is God's desire that our minds are sound.

2 Timothy 1:7 Paul says, God hasn't given us the spirit of fear, but of power and love and of a sound mind.

The second element of the soul is, The will.

Understand God has given each of us free wills. We were created to serve God, but God has given us freedom to make that choice.

Deuteronomy 30:19 I call heaven and earth to record this day against you, that I have set before you, life and death, blessings and cursing, therefore choose life, that both thou and thy seed may live.

Understand God will allow you to go to hell if you will to. Now God clearly tells us his will regarding this, God loves all his creation and doesn't want any-one to spend eternity in hell.

2 Peter 3:19 The Lord is not slack concerning his promises as some men count slackness, but is long-suffering to us ward not willing that any should perish but that all should come to repentance.

Matthew 25:41 Let us know hell was created for the devil and his angels.

That's God's will, but he will not force his will upon us. He wants us to come to a place where we can submit our wills unto him, just as Jesus did in the garden of Gethsemane.

Matthew 26:39 Jesus prayed this prayer, O Father if it be possible let this cup pass from me, never-the-less, not as I will, but as thou will.

Understand, some may have had their wills taken away from them, in cases such as child molestation and rape. Your will was over powered by some-one else lust, but God wasn't behind this, the devil was.

John 10:10 says; The thief (devil) cometh not, but to steal, and to kill, and to destroy.

In cases like this, where your will was taken from you, it is important to forgive. Forgiveness benefits you, maybe in some cases your offender as well, but forgiveness will always benefit you. So many people are not whole in their souls because of offensive. We must forgive those who have offended us and trust God to vindicate you. The word of God says in Luke 17:1,2 (1) It is impossible but that offences will come, but woe (grief) unto him through whom they come. (2) It were better for him that a mil-stone were hanged about his neck and he be cast in the sea, than he should offend one of these little ones. God doesn't take offences lightly, trust him. He tells us to forgive, and he will help you to do just that, but we must be obedient, cooperate with God, he will help you to heal. Pray and be willing to obey. Forgive so you may heal!

The third element of the soul are the emotions.

Emotions are strong feelings, there are negative and positive emotions.

Some negative emotions are, anger and hate.

Negative emotions can be deadly if stored for a long period of time. Let's examine what God's word has to say about these negative emotions.

Anger- Ecclesiastes 7:9 says; Be not hasty in your spirit to be angry, for anger resteth (remains) in the bosom of a fool.

Understand, if you allow anger to remain in you, one may eventually begin to do foolish acts.

Ephesians 4:26 says; Be ye angry and sin not, let not the sun go down on your wrath.

Hate (Hatred) - Proverbs 10:12 Hatred stirreth up strife, but love covereth all sins.

So we see no good thing comes as a result of storing negative emotions!

Now let's look at some positive emotions and what the word has to say. Some positive emotions are, happy and peace.

Happy (Merry) Proverbs 17:22 A merry heart doeth good like a medicine, but a broken spirit drieth the bones.

Peace- Philippians 4:7 And the peace of God which passeth all understanding shall keep your hearts and minds through Christ Jesus.

Understand emotions in itself rather negative or positive are meant to be spontaneous, they are meant to come and go! They are not meant to stay 24/7 especially negative emotions. Negative emotions if stored for a long period of time in the body can be deadly. So these are the 3 elements that makes up the soul, the mind, will and emotions. So how are we to maintain wholeness in our soul? There are 3 components involved. One has to put the word of God into these 3 gates. The eye-gate (read the word) The ear-gate (listen to the word) and the mouth (speak the word) Now I will expound on this in greater detail later on in our lesson, but here is something one should understand about the soul. The heart is a term which also includes one mind, will and emotions. The heart and soul are words that can be used interchangeable, they can be used in the place of one the other. When the heart is mention in the word of God, in the old and new testaments, many times it is referring to one's mind. The Greek word for heart in the New Testament is Kardia. It means mind. The Hebrew word for heart in the old testament is a Hebrew word called Leb. One of its' meaning is the mind also. Now I will be referring to scriptures that uses the word heart coming both from the old and new testament. When the word heart is mention, it is referring to one's mind. With that understanding let's continue our lesson. How can one be whole in their soul?

Proverbs 4:23 says; Keep thy heart with all diligence, for out of it are the issues of life. The living bible states; Above all else guard your hearts, for it effects everything you do. We have the responsibility to guard what goes into our hearts. So how does one accomplish this?

First one must guard what enters these 2 gates, the eyes and the ears, because what comes through these 2 gates can come out of the mouth. One should also put the word of God into these 2 gates as well. The eyes (read the word) the ears (listen to the word) and the mouth will proclaim the word.

Jesus says, Matthew 12:34 Out of the abundance (over-flow) of the heart (kardia) the mouth speaks. You want to know what's in a person heart, listen to what proceeds from the mouth. Understand, what is in the heart comes out of the mouth, but the things that have been seeded in the heart comes through the usage of the eye and ear gate, which then proceeds from the mouth. So the mouth helps to identify what is in the heart.

This is why it is necessary to put the word of God into these gates, the eyes and ears because the word will help you to judge your thought and intentions.

Now here are some things Jesus says that can defile, make you unclean.

Matthew 15:9 Jesus says; For out of the heart proceeds evil thoughts, murders, adulteries, fornication, theft, false witness, blasphemies, these things defile a man. Now one can examine each of these acts and understand that each of these acts first enters the mind by the way of the eye-gate (what is seen) or the ear-gate (what was heard) which then proceeds out of the mouth. The mouth simply identifies what is in the heart!

Let's look at an example using the eye-gate. We will look at the act of adultery.

Matthew 5:28 Jesus says, who-so-ever looketh (eye-gate) on a woman to lust after her hath committed adultery with her already in his heart.

Understand the act of adultery was acted out in the mind of the person, which came through the eye-gate. So one must be careful what enters into these gates, because the mind if not guarded, will meditate on what-ever comes through these gates and if not put in check by the word the actions can be carried out.

Now let's look at another example, this time using the ear-gate

Mark 4:24 Jesus said; Take heed what you hear (ear-gate) with what measure ye mete (measure) it shall be measured to you and unto you that hear shall more be given.

In other-words what you hear is able to come back to you in abundance, reproduce. So be careful what you hear, put the word in (listen to the word)

Understand the word must be sown into the heart (mind), because the word helps to renew the mind.

Ephesians 4:23 And be renewed in the spirit of your mind.

Your spirit becomes born again when you invite Jesus in, but the mind must be renewed by the word so one can take on a new mind set. Understand what you chose to do with the mind, can affect your spirit and body. So as one is guarding the heart, one must put the word into the eye-gate (read the word) into the ear-gate (listen to the word) and your mouth must also proclaim the word.

Now listen to the power of the word. Hebrews 4:12 The word of God is quick (alive) and powerful and sharper than any two-edged sword, piercing even to the dividing asunder of the soul and spirit and of the joints and marrows and is a discerner (judge) of the thoughts and intents of the heart. The word will help you judge your thoughts and intentions. It will help put your thoughts and intentions in check, making sure they are in agreement with the word. Now I want to be sure you are understanding the importance of you taking responsibility to guard your heart, so I am going to share a quick story which I trust will help you understand the importance of guarding the heart.

This story is about 2 men by the names of Sam and Bob who are neighbors.

Sam is a born again believer, how-ever Sam hasn't taken the time to develop a strong spirit. He attends church once a month and that's the only time he hears the word. The only time he prays, is what-ever prayer is offered when he attends church.

Bob on the other hand is not a believer, he has no present interest in the things of God.

Bob how-ever is very annoying. He always has a complaint about something Sam is doing or not doing. Sam has a big dog named Sammy and Bob has a little poodle named Bobbiette. Bob complains that Sam's dog Sammy barks too much and suggests to Sam to keep his dog Sammy in the house. Sam tells Bob it is warm outside and he wants his dog Sammy to play out-doors, he then suggests to Bob, just close your windows. Bob is furious at Sam's suggestion, he goes into his house, Sam goes back into his house and leaves his dog Sammy out to play. Bob comes back out-doors, makes sure Sam isn't looking, he then gives Sam dog Sammy a doggie treat filled with poison. Two hours later Sammy, Sam's dog dies in his backyard. Sam comes out and finds his dog Sammy dead. He then goes over to Bob's house to ask about his dog Sammy. Bob denies all allegations and even offers Sam his condolence, he says, I'm so sorry for your lost. Sam goes back home, knowing Bob has killed his dog Sammy, but he has no way of proving this. Sam now sits in his chair and the process of the soul begins, but remember, you mind does not act without the involvement of the usage of the eye-gate and the ear-gate. Sam is upset because of what he has seen with his eyes (his dead dog) and what he has heard with his ears (Bob's response) so now the process of the soul begins. Sam begins to think (meditate) on how he can get revenge against Bob. Here is his plan, he meditates that on tomorrow, he will get up at 6:00am in the morning. Sam knows Bob let's his little poodle Bobbiette out every morning about 6:15am and leaves her out until about 7:00am.

So Sam plans to be in his backyard at 6:00am He will lay on his roof with his gun which has a silencer on it. When Bobbiette the little poodle comes out, Sam will wait until Bob goes into his house, then shoot Bobbiette and quickly go back into his house. Sam meditates on his plan, his will comes into agreement and says, I hear what you are thinking mind and I will to do it. His emotions now come on board, it is the emotion of anger, it says count me in as well, we will show Bob that he won't get away with this! Sam then goes to bed angry and we understand, the word tells us anger resteth in the bosom of a fool. (Ecclesiastes 7:9) So Sam arises early the next morning and he carries out his foolish plan. He kills Bob little poodle Bobbiette. Understand Sam is a believer, but just hasn't taken the time to renew the mind with the word of God. He didn't have a strong spirit. He had very little word, very little prayer and not much fellowship with other believers. So now this is Sam's end result, because he did not take the time to develop a strong spirit.

Now let's look at this same scenario, only this time, Sam has taken the time to develop a strong spirit. He has taken the time to put the word in and his mind has been renewed. He has listen to the word over and over again, so it has entered the ear-gate, he has personally taken the time to read the word, so it has entered the eye-gate and he constantly speaks or proclaims the word out of his mouth. So the word has taken root in the heart, and he can now bear fruit. So let's begin our story once more, but this time Sam has a strong spirit.

Bob has killed Sam's dog Sammy. Sam sits and meditates on what Bob has done to his dog. A thought comes to mind to kill Bob's dog Bobbiette, but Sam begins to speak the word out of his mouth aloud. He says, God your word says vengeance is yours, and you will repay (Romans 12:19) Your word says, in (Psalms 37:1,2) Fret not thyself because of evil doers, neither be thou envious against the workers of iniquity. For they shall soon be cut down like the grass and wither as the green herb. So Sam then falls on his face and begins to pray for Bob's salvation.

Understand there is a difference when we take time to properly guard our hearts. Many issues will arise, but we must be ready to respond the correct way! So we understand to be whole in our souls (mind, will and emotions) we must guard our minds and there are 3 components involved in doing so, they are, we must put the word into these 2 gates. Eye-gate (read the word) Ear-gate (listen to the word) and the mouth must proclaim the word. Applying these three components consistently will help us guard our hearts which will help us to stay whole in our souls.

Remember (living bible) Proverbs 4:23 Above all else guard your hearts for it effects everything you do. So let's do a quick review of what we have studied thus far, we understand God desires the totality of our beings whole, spirit, soul and body. We said to be strong in our spirits, 3 components are involved, they are... (1) Attend a local assembly (2) Study the word (3) Spend time in prayer. One should practice these 3 things on a consistent base.

We understand for one to be whole in their souls 3 Components are involved as well, they are... Put the word into these 3 gates, the eye-gate (read the word) Ear-gate (listen to the word) The mouth (speak, proclaim the word) Understand, one must practice putting the word into these 3 gates on a consistent base, because you don't want to just become whole, you want to remain whole.

Now let's lastly examine how to be whole in your body. Remember if you want to participate in doing exploits (notable deeds for the kingdom) one should seek to become strong in all 3 areas. The Spirit, Soul and Body! Let's talk about the body.

The body make up consist of 3 elements as well, they are… Flesh, Bone and Blood

Leviticus 17:11 For the life of the flesh is in the blood.

The blood gives life to your flesh. Now the body is different from the spirit and the soul, although all three parts of your being are closely connected. In Luke 24:39 Jesus appeared to his disciples after he had risen from the dead. He was in his body. When his disciples first saw him they were afraid, because they thought he was a spirit. Jesus tells them behold my hands and feet that it is I myself, handle me and see, for a spirit hath not flesh and bones as you see me have. Remember, we are really spirit beings. Our spirits will live on eternally, but we determine where our spirits will exist by the decision we make while living in the earth. If one chose to receive Jesus into their life.

1 Corinthians 6:19,20 Paul says,

> 19 What know ye not that your body is the temple (house) of the holy ghost which is in you, which ye have of God and you are not your own.

> 20 For you are bought with a price, therefore glorify (honor) God in your body and your spirit, which are God's.

So how can we keep our bodies strong (whole) so we may glorify God in these bodies?

There are 3 components involved, but first here is something I want you to understand about the body. The body is a physical (natural) body, so we will talk about physical things to maintain our physical bodies. Now here are 3 components needed to keep our bodies strong.

Proper diet

Proper exercise

Proper rest

Now understand in this particular lesson, I will not specify what you are to eat or what you should not eat, but I will say this, under the old covenant the children of Israel abided by the Levitical law found in Leviticus Chapter 11. Here it specified what animals was clean and unclean. We are now living under a new covenant and Romans 14:2-3 tells us we are not to judge a person on what they eat. In other words, don't juge their diets.

1Timothy 4:4,5 says,

4 For every creature of God is good and not to be refused if it be received with thanksgiving.

5 For it is sanctify by the word of God and prayer.

How-ever the word of God does tell us in 1 Corinthians 11:31 We do have the responsibility to judge ourselves. If one chose to eat according to the Levitical law found in Leviticus Chapter 11, they have not sinned and there would be nothing wrong with doing so. What I encourage people to do is this, we are to take caring for our bodies very seriously, become educated, because you only get one body to carry out your purpose, so taking care of the body is very important!

This body belong to God, one can have much intellect or one can be highly anointed by God, but if the physical house breaks down, everything is put on hold! So pray and ask God to give you wisdom and knowledge how to take care of this body. Hosea 4:6 My people are destroyed for the lack of knowledge.

Now I have asked God for knowledge regarding my physical body and he has given me wisdom and knowledge. Many years ago I had put my children down for a nap. I then heard the holy-spirit speak so plainly, he said the devil desires to kill you through your eating habits. This was a wake -up call for me. I begin seeking God for wisdom and knowledge how to care for my body.

I had another experience I will not forget; this was also many years ago. I had a boil on the back of my neck. I wasn't sure what it was until the holy-spirit identified what it was. I was praying asking God to heal me. The holy spirit spoke, he identified the problem. He told me it was a boil, he then asked me a question, he said, how did I tell you to eat? I pause for a moment, and the holy spirit brought back to my mind, two weeks prior to this event he had told me to eat vegetables and drink water only. I quickly dismissed that thought because I didn't want to do this. I later repented for my disobedience. Now God did heal me, but it was not by the means of the supernatural. I obeyed what he had instructed me to do earlier, I ate vegetables and drunk water only for about two weeks and the boil completely left!

This was my beginning of seeking out knowledge how to care for my physical body. Now God spoke to me later and said, he could have healed me supernatural, but if I had continued to eat the same foods that was responsible for the condition I had suffered, I would later, down the road eventually experience the same problem. Hosea 4:6 says; My people are destroyed for lack of knowledge.

Now let's talk about the 3 components involved in keeping the body strong (whole)

3 John 1:2 Beloved, I wish above all things that thou prosper and be in health, even as thy soul prospereth.

Component 1

One must eat a proper diet. In the book of Daniel, Chapter 1:3-5 you will find a story about a Babylonian king by the name of Nebuchadnezzar. This king ordered his servant Ashpenaz who was in charge of all the eunuchs to hire some employees from among the tribe of Juda. Now these young men had been taken captive and were from the royal seed of the tribe of Judah. Now here are the kings' specifications for his employees. (1) He wanted youth who had no blemish, so they had to be young and good looking. (2)

He wanted men who were skillful in wisdom and understanding science. So they had to be very intelligent, sharp guys. (3) He wanted employees that had ability in them to stand in the king's palace, so they had to be already groomed to work in the king's palace, they had to know how to carry themselves around royalty. Now if his candidates met all of these qualifications, they were then taught the language of the Chaldeans and then given a special diet. Understand, they just couldn't put anything into their bodies. Now why do you suppose the king was concerned about his employee diet? Wasn't it enough that they had met all of the other specifications of the king? They were young, good looking, intelligent, already groomed to carry themselves in the king's palace and had learned the king's language.

This king evidently deemed himself and his business to be very important. He took it very serious. His thinking probably was, I am satisfied with all the specification they have met, but if they bodies break down, this would mean there would be sick days, which would then interrupt his business from being carried out in a timely fashion. Now this was natural king who thought of his business as a serious matter. We are all called to work for the king of kings, The Lord Jesus Christ! We all have been given the assignment of reconciling souls unto Christ. The ministry of reconciliation, according to 2Corinthians 5:18. Don't you think God takes his work serious as well, and he is concern how we take care of our physical house. Eating properly will help your body to function more efficiently. Read the entire chapter of Daniel chapter 1 and you will find Daniel and the 3 Hebrews

boys requested a special diet aside from what the king had ordered, because the food had been offered up to idols. The word says they were found to be ten times better than their peers. So eating the proper food will help your bodies to function more effectively.

So to be strong in your physical body (whole), component number 1 is, one must eat a proper diet.

Component 2

One must get proper exercise. 1 Timothy 4:8 says, Bodily exercise profiteth little, but godliness is profitable unto all things having promise of the life that now is, and of that which is to come.

(Amp. Ver.) For physical training is of some value (useful little) but godliness (spiritual training) is useful and of value in everything and in every-way, for it holds promise for the present life and also for the life which is to come. Paul is saying here that the discipline one uses to exercise their physical bodies, one must apply that same discipline even more so to exercise themselves spiritually. We must discipline ourselves in both the spiritual and physical realm. Now although Paul says there is little profit in exercising our physical bodies, there is still profit there, but one must be aware that exercise without godly living profits little.

Matthew 16:26 says; What is a man profit if he should gain the whole world and lose his own soul? Or what will a man give in exchange for his soul?

So we see to maintain wholeness in the body, we have thus far (1) Proper Diet, (2) Proper Exercise, Let's look at component number 3.

Component 3

One must seek to get proper rest. Matthew 11:28, 29

> 28 Jesus said; Come unto me all that labor and are heavy laden (burden) and I will give you rest.

> 29 Take my yoke upon you and learn of me, for I am meek and lowly in heart and you will find rest unto your souls.

It is important to make sure our bodies have an adequate amount of rest. Jesus even took out time to make sure he and his disciples had an adequate amount of rest.

Mark 6:31 says, And he (Jesus) said unto them (disciples) come ye yourselves apart into a desert place and rest a while, for there were many coming and going and they had no leisure (free time) so much as to eat.

Now God intends for our bodies to have rest as well. Here are some promises he has made regarding rest.

Proverb 3:24 Your sleep will be sweet.

Proverb 127:3 He gives his beloved sleep.

Ecclesiastes 5:21a The sleep of a laboring man is sweet. (sound)

So these are the 3 components that will help us maintain healthy bodies. They are, (1) Proper diet (2) Proper exercise (3) Proper Rest. Understand it is important that these three components are applied to one lives on a consistent base, because God doesn't want us to stop short at becoming whole, he wants us to maintain being whole.

Jesus made use of these 3 components, he took time to eat properly, his diet sometimes included broiled fish. (Luke 24:42) He took time to exercise, in that particular era many walked just about everywhere they had to go accept the wealthy, who rode in chariots or when individuals were traveling a long period of time, people then used ships and boats. Jesus also took time to rest as we have already looked at in Mark 6:31 So we see Jesus used these 3 components as well. His assignment in the earth was very important and he took it very seriously and so should we!

Now let's review how to maintain wholeness for the total you, one last time.

For the spirit there are 3 components involved, they are,

1. Join a local assembly (attend on a consistent base)

2. Study of the word (consistent base)

3. Pray (consistent base)

For the soul 3 components are involved, they are, one must guard the heart and to do this one must put the word into these 3 gates.

1. The eye-gate (read the word) consistent base.

2. The ear-gate (listen to the word) consistent base.

3. The mouth (speak the word) consistent base.

For the body 3 components are involved, they are

proper diet (consistent base)

proper exercise (consistent base)

proper rest (consistent base)

Remember, God desires the totality of your being whole, spirit, soul and body. So if you want to do exploits for the kingdom of God, one should seek to be whole in each of these areas and one should then maintain the wholeness they have obtained, which will require consistency!

Lesson 5

THE POWER OF THE WORD AND GOD'S HEALING PROMISE

Why do you suppose Job stated in Job 23:12 Neither have I gone back from the commandments of his lips, I have esteemed the words of his (God) mouth more than my necessary food.

Gods' words were very valuable unto Job. He understood the power of God's word. Let's study the secrets Job came to understand about the word of God.

In Genesis 1:1-3 It states, how heaven and earth begin.

> 1 In the beginning God created the heaven and the earth.
>
> 2 And the earth was without form and void and darkness was upon the face of the deep. And the spirit of God moved upon the face of the waters.
>
> 3 And God said, (his word) let there be light, and there was light.

Everything in heaven and earth begun by God speaking his powerful word. One word from God can change a nation. That's how powerful God's word is.

Now let's further examine the power of God's word

1. Joshua 1:8 This book of the law (God's word) shall not depart out of thy mouth, but thou shalt meditate there-in day and night that thou mayest observe to do according to all that is written there-in. For then thou shall make thou way prosperous and then thou shalt have good success.

   God's word is powerful enough to prosper you and bring good success.

2. Psalms 1:1-3

   1 Blessed in the man that walketh not in the counsel of the ungodly, nor standeth in the way of sinners, nor sitteth in the seat of the scornful

   2 But his delight is in the law (word) of the Lord, and in his law (word) doth he meditate day and night.

   3 And he shall be like a tree planted by the rivers of water that bringeth forth his fruit in his season, his leaf also shall not wither and whatsoever he doeth shall prosper.

   The word is powerful enough to bring stability and prosperity.

4. Psalms 107:20- He sent his word, and healed them, and delivered them from their destructions.

   The word is powerful enough to bring healing and deliverance.

5. Psalms 119:89- Forever O Lord, thy word is settled in the heavens.

   God's word is powerful and sure, it stands firm in the heavens.

6. Proverbs 4:20-22

   20 My son, attend to my words, incline thine ear unto my sayings.

21 Let them not depart from thine eyes, keep them in the midst of thine heart.

22 For they are life unto those that find them, and health to all their flesh.

God's word is powerful enough to work like medicine, only with no side effects.

7. Isaiah 55:11- So shall my word be that goeth forth out of my mouth, it shall not return unto void, but it shall accomplish that which I please, and it shall prosper in the thing where to I sent it.

God's word goes out of his mouth with a assignment attach to it, and it is powerful enough to fulfill that assignment.

8. Jeremiah 1:12

Then saith the Lord unto me, thou has well seen. For I will hasten my word to perform it.

God's word is powerful and God is alert and active watching over his word to perform it.

9. Matthew 24:35

Heaven and earth shall pass away, but my words shall not pass away.

God's word is not only powerful, but also eternal.

10. Hebrews 4:12

12 For the word of God is quick (alive) and powerful, and sharper than any two edged sword, piercing even to the dividing asunder of the soul and spirit and the joints and marrow, and is a discerner of the thoughts and intents of the heart.

God's word is powerful, it is able to divide things that are closely connected and will help you judge your thoughts and intentions.

So we see the power God's word carries. This is what Job understood. Let's now examine the immutability of his word and the reputation of the God who has spoken the word.

Numbers 23:19

> God is not a man, that he should lie, neither the son of man that he should repent, hath he spoken, and shall he not make it good?

So understand, God's word is powerful, and he stands by his word. Let's examine some healing promises made by God, because God is a covenant keeping God. (1 Kings 8:23)

Healing Promises

1. Psalms 89:34- My covenant will I not break, nor alter the thing that is gone out of my lips.

2. Exodus 23:25,26- 25 And ye shall serve the Lord your God and he shall bless thy bread, and water, and I will take sickness away from the midst of thee.

    26 There shall nothing cast their young (no miscarriages) nor be barren in thy land, the number of thy days I will fulfill.

3. 1 Kings 8:56- Blessed be the Lord, that hath given rest unto his people Israel, according to all that he promised, there hath not failed one word of all his good promise, which he promised by the hand of Moses his servant. (God is a covenant keeping God, he is not a respecter of person, what he has done for Israel, he will do for you)

4. Psalms 147:3- He healeth the broken in heart, and bindeth up their wounds.

5. Isaiah 40:31- But they that wait upon the Lord, shall renew their strength, they shall mount up with wings as eagles; they shall run and not be weary; and they shall walk, and not faint. (God will strengthen you as you wait upon him)

6. Isaiah 41:13- For I the Lord thy God will hold thy right hand, saying unto thee, fear not, I will help thee.

7. Isaiah 53:4,5- Surely he hath borne our griefs, and carried our sorrows, yet we did esteem him stricken, smitten of God, and afflicted.

    But he was wounded for our transgression, he was bruised for our iniquities, the chastisement of our peace was upon him, and with his stripes we are healed.

8. Jeremiah 30:17- For I will restore health unto thee, and I will heal thee of thy wounds, saith the Lord.

9. Nahum 1:9- What do ye imagine against the Lord? He will make an utter end: affliction shall not rise up the second time.

10. Matthew 18:18,19- 18 Verily I say unto you, whatsoever ye shall bind on earth, shall be bound in heaven and whatsoever ye shall loose on earth, shall be loosed in heaven.

    19 Again I say unto you, that if two of you shall agree on earth, as touching anything that they shall ask, it shall be done for them of my father which is in heaven.

11. Matthew 21:22- And all things whatsoever ye shall ask in prayer believing, ye shall receive.

12. Mark 9:23- If thou canst believe, all things are possible to him that believeth.

13. Mark 10:27- And Jesus looking upon them saith, with men it is impossible, but not with God, For with God all things are possible.

14. Mark 16:17,18- 17 And these signs shall follow them that believe; in my name shall they cast out devils, they shall speak with new tongues;

    18 They shall take up serpents; and if they drink any deadly thing it shall not hurt them, they shall lay hands on the sick, and they shall recover.

15. Luke 10:19- Behold, I give unto power to tread on serpents and scorpions, and over all the power of the enemy, and nothing shall by any means hurt you.

16. James 5:14,15- 14 Is any sick among you? Let him call the elders of the church, and let them pray over him, anointing him with oil in the name of the Lord.

    15 And the prayer of faith shall save the sick, and the Lord shall raise him up; and if he have committed sins, they shall be forgiven him.

17. Philippians 1:6- Being confident of this very thing, that he which hath begun a good work in you will perform it until the day of Jesus Christ.

18. 1 John 5:14,15- 14 And this is the confidence that we have in him, that, if we ask anything according to his will, he heareth us;

    15 And if we know that he hears us, whatsoever we ask, we know that we have the petitions that we desired of him.

19. 3 John 1:2- Beloved I wish above all things that thou mayest prosper and be in health, even as thy soul prospereth.

20. 2 Corinthians 1:20- For all the promises of God in him are yea (yes) and in him amen (so be it) unto the glory of God by us.

    So we see God's promises are sure, and God is a covenant keeping God.

Let's pray, we understand the power of God's word, and the promises he has made to us. We will now speak to mountains that desires to stand between you and God's promises. We will command the mountains to be removed.

Mark 11:23- For verily I say unto you, that whosoever shall say unto this mountain, be thou removed, and be thou cast into the sea, and shall not doubt in his heart, but shall believe that those things which he saith shall come to pass, he shall have whatsoever he saith.

So Father in Jesus name, we speak to all mountains of sickness and diseases, we command them to be removed in Jesus name.

1. We speak to, acid reflux, heart burn, we command you to go in Jesus name.

2. We speak to all forms of addictions; we command you to be broken in Jesus name. We speak to, drug addictions, nicotine addictions, alcoholism addictions, sexual addictions, we break your powers now in Jesus name. We command all cravings to cease in Jesus name.

3. We speak to, all forms of allergies, we command you to cease now, clear up in Jesus name.

4. We speak to, all forms of arthritis, that desires to cripple God's people, we command you to go in Jesus name. We address, joint pains, shoulder pain, back pain, hip pain, pain in hands, leg pain, and wherever else the spirit of arthritis may lodge, we command you to come out in Jesus name.

5. We speak to all forms of blood disorders; we command you to cease in Jesus name. we address, sickle cell anemia, aids, leukemia, high blood pressure, low blood pressure, high blood sugar, low blood sugar, poor blood circulation, we command your blood to regulate now in Jesus name, be normal.

6. We speak to attention deficit, we address autism, we command you to cease now in Jesus name. We say you will focus without any further distraction.

7. We speak to all forms of breathing disorders; we command you to clear up now in Jesus name. We address, asthma, bronchitis, go in Jesus name.

8. We speak to all forms of back pain; we command backs to be whole in Jesus name. Curved spines, straighten up in Jesus name.

9. We speak to all forms of cancer; we command you to go in Jesus name. We curse you to the very root, we address, brain cancer, breast cancer, colon cancer, cervical cancer, liver cancer, lung cancer, ovarian cancer, pancreatic cancer, prostate cancer, we command you to come out in Jesus name.

10. We speak to cerebral palsy; we command you to go in Jesus name.

11. We speak to all cholesterol levels; we command you to be normal in Jesus name. We address, high cholesterol, low cholesterol, we say adjust in Jesus name, be normal.

12. We speak to the spirit of diabetes; we command to go in Jesus name. we say blood sugar regulate in Jesus name.

13. We speak to all forms of digestive disorders; we command you to go in Jesus name.

14. We speak to all forms of dizziness; we command you to cease in Jesus name. We address the condition of vertigo; we say cease in Jesus name.

15. We speak to all forms of eating disorders; we command you to go in Jesus name. We address, anorexia, bulimia, compulsive eating, we say cease in Jesus name.

16. We speak to all forms of eye problems; we command you to clear up in Jesus name. We address, cataracts, glaucoma, we say go in Jesus name.

17. We speak to the spirit of fear; we command you to lose the minds of God's people in Jesus name. We address, panic attacks, nervous conditions, night mares, cease in Jesus name. We speak soundness to every mind in Jesus name.

18. We speak to all forms of feet disorders; we command you to go in Jesus name. We address, bunions, gout, all kinds of fungus, we say cease in Jesus name.

19. We speak to all forms of headaches; we command you to cease in Jesus name. We address migraines, go in Jesus name.

20. We speak to all forms of hearing conditions; we command ears to be whole in Jesus name. We address, the spirit of deafness, ringing ears, ear infections, we say be whole in Jesus name.

21. We speak to all forms of heart problems; we command the heart to function normal in Jesus name. We address, clogging of the arteries, congestive heart failure, all form of heart failures, we say cease in Jesus name.

22. We speak to the condition of infertility, bareness, we command wombs to open up now in Jesus name, and we say timely births come forth in Jesus name. We cancel miscarriages, premature births, we say no more in Jesus name.

23. We speak to all kind of infections, we command you to be dispelled from the bodies. We address, influenza, sinusitis infections, boils, cysts, gum infections. We say go in Jesus name.

24. We speak to kidney disorders; we command your kidneys to function normal in Jesus name.

25. We speak to laryngitis, we command you to lose all vocal chords, in Jesus name. We say vocal chords be strong in Jesus name.

26. We speak to all, losses of taste, losses of smell, losses of feelings, we command your senses to be restored in Jesus name.

27. We speak to the spirit of lupus, we command you to leave the body in Jesus name.

28. We speak to all kinds of memory lost, we command your memory to be restored in Jesus name. We address, Alzheimer's, amnesia, dementia, we say lose the minds and we speak soundness of mind to God's people in Jesus name.

29. We speak to all forms of mental illness; we command you go from the minds in Jesus. We address, schizophrenia, bipolar, we speak soundness to your mind in Jesus name.

30. We speak to nose bleed; we command you to cease now in Jesus name.

31. We speak to conditions of seizures, epilepsy, we command you to cease in Jesus name.

32. We speak to all forms of sexual diseases; we command you to go from the bodies in Jesus name. We address, all forms of herpes, gonorrhea, go in Jesus name.

33. We speak to shingles; we command you to go in Jesus name.

34. We speak to all forms of skin disorders; we command you to clear up in Jesus name. We address, skin lumps, warts, eczema, skin cancer, acne, we say go in Jesus name.

35. We speak to all forms of sleep disorders; we command you to lose the minds in Jesus name. We address, insomnia, sleep apnea, restlessness, we say go in Jesus name; We say your sleep will be sweet from this night forward.

36. We speak to the spirit of suicide, we command you to be broken in Jesus name, we address the spirit of depression, we command you to be broken in the name of Jesus.

37. We speak to all forms of stomach disorders; we command you to cease now in Jesus name. We address, ulcers, bladder infections, diarrhea, we say clear up in Jesus name.

38. We speak to all forms of thyroid conditions, we command high thyroid, low thyroid, we say regulate in Jesus name.

39. We speak to tonsillitis; we command you to clear up in Jesus name.

40. We speak to all form of tumors; we command you to go in Jesus name. We address, brain tumors, cysts, go now in Jesus name.

Now Father, in Jesus name, I thank you for your healing power that is present to heal. I thank you, your healing power settles over the bodies and minds of your people in Jesus name.

We praise you these afflictions shall not rise up a second time.

I call forth missing limbs, I say come forth in Jesus name. I call forth missing eyes, I call you forth back into the eye sockets in Jesus name. I command blind eyes to open up in Jesus name. I command deaf ears to be open, the dumb to begin to speak, in Jesus name.

Father I thank you, those who have died prematurely are now being raised up to life again, in Jesus name. We praise you for all the notable signs, wonders and miracles that follows as a result of using the powerful name of Jesus.

Now we encourage you to do what you could not do!

BIOGRAPHY

Apostle Gloria Johnson is a born again believer. She is married to Apostle Kenneth Johnson. They are the founders of Tav school of ministry. Together they have two sons, Emmanuel and Gabriel, two daughters in law, and five grandsons.

Apostle Gloria mandate from God is to help equip his people for the work which they are called. To accomplish this, she uses venues such as; Tav school of ministry, churches, retreats, seminars and conferences. She is equipped by the gifts God has placed in her, which are; that of a psalmist, a teacher, a healing, a deliverance and prophetic anointing. Gloria's heart desire is to see God's people become mature in him, walking in love and unity with one the other.

Other classes taught by Apostle Gloria are; The school of purpose, The school of prophets, The school of evangelism, The school of Naomi and Ruth and The school of the spirit.

To contact Apostle Gloria Johnson, use the following information;

Tav Ministries P.O. Box 6333 Douglasville Georgia 30154
Tav school of ministry.org
770 771 5141

Printed in the United States
By Bookmasters